What other experts are saying about *Finding Your New Owner*:

"Finally a book that is loaded with optimism on a subject that confuses, confounds and eludes legions of business owners. Accessible in its language and layout, *Finding Your New Owner* leads business owners through a straightforward and practical process to plan and implement their toughest and most important event -- their business ownership transition. We know that the Baby Boomer generation has been the greatest wealth creation generation in the history of mankind. Whether this generation of entrepreneurs can now do their last deal -- their toughest deal -- and honour themselves, their risk taking and sacrifice, is Jack Beauregard's personal mission. Above all else, his new book shows that with some dedication to basic planning principles, a business owner's legacy can be rich, profound and majestic -- a testament to a life well-lived, both during and after the transition of their business".

Tom Deans Ph.D. – award winning speaker and author of the bestselling book *Every Family's Business*

"I have sadly observed too many business founders who bury themselves, almost literally, in their companies, never pausing to consider what the ultimate consequences will be for their family and employees when they pass away. In *Finding Your New Owner* Jack Beauregard brightly illuminates another path--one which is much more rewarding in all respects. It is a purposeful journey through the transition from success as a business owner to significance as a family and community leader. I highly recommend this book to anyone who wants to find meaning and fulfillment in the second half of life".

John A. Warnick – Founder of *The Purposeful Planning Institute* and Estate Planning attorney

"*Finding Your New Owner* is a must-read for any business owner and his or her spouse or significant other. The book makes sense and is a call to action. I will certainly be recommending it to my clients."

Jerry Socol – Founder of The Socol Group and five-time CEO including a $900 million public company

"In my work as an Executive/Leadership Coach, I have become keenly aware of how unprepared most business owners are regarding life after transitioning out of their business. This book gives the reader a practical, step-by-step approach about how to manage the transition process both emotionally and professionally. The exercises will help the business owner conceptualize the steps needed to have a satisfying and financially secure life moving forward."

Linda Cohan, MSW, CSC – Executive/Leadership Coach

"In *Finding Your New Owner*, Jack Beauregard shares with sensitivity and unique insight the steps required for transitioning yourself away from your business. For those who are struggling with what to do next with their life, Jack offers a wealth of ideas and a step-by-step approach to figuring it out and making it happen. Every boomer business owner should read this book!"

Wayne Vanwyck – Founder & CEO of The Achievement Centre International and author of *The Business Transition Crisis: Plan Your Succession Now and Beat the Biggest Business Selloff in History*

"This book helps business owners ask the tough questions and forces them to work ON their business, not just IN it. A great read with long-term impact!"

Paige Arnof-Fenn – Founder & CEO of Mavens & Moguls

FINDING YOUR NEW OWNER:

FOR YOUR BUSINESS, FOR YOUR LIFE

A GUIDE TO A NEW PARADIGM FOR BABY BOOMER BUSINESS OWNERS

BY JACK BEAUREGARD

STPI PRESS

Published by:
STPI Press
Successful Transition Planning Institute
One Mifflin Place, Harvard Square
Cambridge, Massachusetts 02138
www.successfultransitionplanning.com

Publisher's Cataloguing-in-Publication Data

Beauregard, Jack
Finding Your New Owner: For Your Business, For Your Life / Jack Beauregard / Cambridge MA / STPI Press, 2011.

p.;cm.

ISBN 978-0-9836311-1-8
ISBN 978-0-9836311-0-1

1. Sale of business enterprises. 2. Baby boom generation -- Retirement. 3. Retirement planning.
4. Family-owned business enterprises. 5. Self-realization. I. Title.

Printed in the United States of America.

Contents

iii **Acknowledgements**

PART I **Who Wants To Retire? Not Me**

3 Chapter 1
Why You Don't Want to Think about Leaving Your Company

20 Chapter 2
Fifteen Ways to Leave Your Company Unsuccessfully – and How to Avoid Them

34 Chapter 3
The Head and Heart of an Owner: A Strategic Approach to Creating a New Future for Your Business and Yourself

PART II **How To Create A New Future You Can't Wait To Live**

53 Chapter 4
From Being CEO of Your Company to Becoming CEO of Your Life

62 Chapter 5
It's Not "Retirement," It's "The Platinum Years[SM]" – a New Stage of Active Life for Baby Boomers

69 Chapter 6
Why Your Personal Transition Plan Is the Essential First Step for a Successful Business Transition

PART III **How To Create A Successful Business Transition That Will Bring You A New Life Of Meaning And Purpose**

93 Chapter 7
Thinking Like a CEO

102 Chapter 8
Expanding Your Thinking about the Transition Process

114 Chapter 9
Expanding Your Thinking about Your Options for New Ownership

140 Chapter 10
Expanding Your Thinking about the Future of Your Company

156 Chapter 11
Your Collaborative "Dream Team": Working Together to Help You Achieve Your Goals

175 Chapter 12
Finding Your New Owner: A Head and Heart Approach

185 Additional Resources & Client Testimonials

192 Ordering Information

Acknowledgements

I would like to thank the many people who helped make this book possible:

Paul Cronin, my business partner in STPI's development, for his extraordinary networking and social media skills and his strategic vision which have helped bring STPI's ideas out to the world, nationally and internationally, and has brought so many talented individuals into association with STPI.

Joe Cloutre, Ken Halkin, Steve Stanganelli, and the MetroWest Business Advisors team of Michael Corrigan, Armand Diarbekirian and John Lawlor – skilled advisors who contributed some of the case studies in this book.

The many owners I've worked with over the years – for the privilege of working with them, for their courage in dealing with both the Head and Heart issues of transitioning out of their companies, and from whom I've learned so much about the potential for growth within each of us.

Steve Harris and Jed Cohen, for their continued faith in this work.

William Entwistle III, Harvey Wigder and Kevin Long, for their intelligence and creativity in helping move this work forward.

The amazingly gifted design and project management team at SMDmarketing – Susan Doré, Leanne Gillespie and Brandy Joyner – for their fantastic work in designing the beautiful cover and text layout for this book.

Paige Arnof-Fenn, Linda Cohan, Jerry Socol, Tom Deans, John A. Warnick and Wayne Vanwyck for their feedback, comments and suggestions for the manuscript.

John Leonetti of Pinnacle Equity Solutions, Dave Poulin of Morgan Stanley Smith Barney, and Mark Newton and Dan Hicks of Principal Financial Group for understanding and appreciating STPI's mission.

And finally, my deepest appreciation to my wife and soulmate Maureen, for her ongoing loving support and her faith in me and my work for 18 years.

WHO WANTS TO RETIRE? NOT ME!

CHAPTER 1

Why You Don't Want to Think about Leaving Your Company

If you don't want to think about retiring, I don't blame you. There are plenty of reasons for not changing what you have now.

You've probably heard about other owners who sold their businesses and retired – and after a few months they became bored and depressed.

You like running your company, you're good at what you do, and maybe it's hard for you to imagine what you'd do with your life if you didn't have that workplace to go to every day.

Right now, your company is your life.

But maybe you also have some ideas of what you could do if the responsibility of running your company didn't take so much of your time and energy.

Maybe you have some thoughts or dreams of what you could be doing instead.

- Maybe you want to spend more time with your family, especially your grandchildren.
- Maybe you have a hobby or favorite recreational activity that you'd like to devote more time to.
- Maybe you'd like to expand your intellectual horizons, take some college classes in literature or history or philosophy. Or maybe you'd like to develop and express your creative side in a new way.
- Maybe you and your spouse have talked about traveling to different parts of the world – but you never had the time to do it.
- Maybe there's a volunteer program, a favorite cause or community concern that you'd like to become more involved with. There are a lot of things you could do with your life, if you weren't so busy running your company.

Or maybe some big company has recently offered to buy your business, and if you sell it, you're going to have to think seriously about what you will do with the rest of your life.

For whatever reason, maybe you've been thinking about the possibility of leaving your company and moving on. But at the same time, you feel uneasy about the prospect of making such a momentous change in your life.

For many years you've been the successful CEO of your own company. Now you are facing a new challenge – a future in which you may have to make a major business and personal transition.

This book explains what this challenge involves and how you can meet it successfully. It will show you how you can successfully move from being CEO of your company, to becoming CEO of your new life.

You already know how to think strategically about running your business – that's what made you so successful as a business owner. This book explains how you can think strategically – step-by-step – about how to successfully transfer your company to new ownership, on your terms, so the transition meets your business, financial and personal objectives. And it will show you how to strategically create a new life that you can't wait to live.

~~~~~

Here are the stories of five owners who were facing the challenge of transition.

1. Peter A. - the fifty-something owner of a law firm that employed another full-time attorney, a part-time attorney and three paralegals, decided that he was going to retire when his current office lease came to term. Although it was assumed that one of the other attorneys would take over ownership of the practice, no formal plans had been made. When Peter's financial advisor asked if he wanted to make formal plans for who would succeed him as the new owner, Peter didn't want to discuss the issue and had no interest in
~~~~~

implementing any of his advisor's suggestions. Then Peter developed a serious health problem and had to leave the firm unexpectedly. Without any kind of advance planning, his colleague was unable to secure suitable financing to keep the firm going. As a result, Peter had to close his company, assume the cost of outstanding equipment leases and ended up laying-off four employees.

2. Sean B. - was a pharmacist who had built up a good local business. He raised his family well and his kids all became success stories. Sean worked 70-80 hours per week and had little time for outside interests. When he reached his sixties he decided to sell his store to a large chain. Since the chain no longer needed him, Sean was on his own with nothing to do for the first time in his adult life. He had no hobbies, but because he knew a lot about medicine, he spent the rest of his life focused on managing his various aches, pains and illnesses – less than an ideal "retirement."

3. Richard C. - the co-owner of a company that manufactured medical devices, decided to retire and sold his company to his partner. Richard's plan was to move to South Carolina, to an upscale community adjoining a country club, where he intended to buy and run some local business in order to give him something to do in his retirement. However, he soon discovered that there were no suitable business opportunities available in his new location. With nothing else to do, Richard's new life ended up boring and unsatisfying.

4. Fred D. - who owned a successful food distribution company in Massachusetts, was approached by a large company in the same field that wanted to purchase his business. Since the potential buyer was offering him a good financial settlement, Fred decided that this would be a good time to retire. He realized however that he had no idea what he wanted to do in his new life.

   Then Fred discovered that there was a way to think strategically about his new future so he could create a fulfilling new life for himself. After exploring what he really wanted to do in his new life, Fred created a comprehensive plan for his future that included many of his favorite outdoor activities. Now he is following the plan he created for his new life, and is enjoying it immensely. His life is filled with enjoyable activities such as hiking and canoeing, and he couldn't be happier.

5. John E. - co-owner of a successful heating, ventilation and air conditioning equipment company in upstate New York, was trying to decide whether or not to sell his share in the company and retire. He realized that he needed to think about more than how to get the best financial outcome when leaving. He also did not want to begin the actual business transition process until he had first created a personal plan for what he was going to do in his new life.

John discovered that there was a way to think strategically about both his business and personal futures, so he could leave his company successfully and move into a fulfilling new life. After becoming aware of and exploring both his business and personal options, he created a plan for how he would transition out of the company on his terms, and a plan for his personal life in which he could engage in activities that were personally meaningful to him, including doing part-time consulting, fishing in the local lakes, and giving back to the local community through volunteer activities that appealed to him. With his personal and business transition plans in hand, John was ready to sell his company and move on to his new life.

In these case studies, the names and other identifying information have been changed to respect privacy.

Why were the first three owners unsuccessful in responding to the challenge of personal and business transition? Because they didn't know that there was a way to think about leaving their companies successfully and creating dynamic, interesting new futures for their lives.

Why were the last two owners able to respond successfully to the challenge of transition? Because they learned to think strategically about how they wanted to leave their companies and what they wanted to do in their new lives.

Helping You Discover Clarity, Opportunity, Meaning and Purpose

For 15 years I've been helping business owners who are going through various kinds of business and personal transitions. Fred and John, in the last two stories above, used the methods I created for a successful transition process.

The old model known as "retirement" is inappropriate for Baby Boomers. Because of our unique history and accomplishments, Baby Boomers in their 50s and 60s are getting ready to move into a new stage of active life, that can go on for another 10, 20 or 30 years.

My own background as the successful CEO of a multi-million dollar company lets me understand what it means to be a business owner. And my long involvement in teaching businesspeople and other organizational leaders how to expand their thinking to increase both personal and business success, led me to develop a unique process for helping business owners discover how they could successfully transition both their companies and themselves to a rewarding new future.

I founded STPI, the Successful Transition Planning Institute, to teach this unique approach not only to Baby Boomer business owners, but also to their professional advisors, so their advisors could help the business owners they work with transition successfully.

STPI's unique approach to planning for the transition process is reflected in the four cardinal points of our "Successful Transition Planning Compass," which is designed to help you, the business owner, gain **C**larity in thinking about your personal and business futures so you can discover new **O**pportunities for yourself and your company, and create new sources of **M**eaning and **P**urpose in your new future. (See Figure 1-A.)

Figure 1-A

STPI's "Successful Transition Planning Compass"

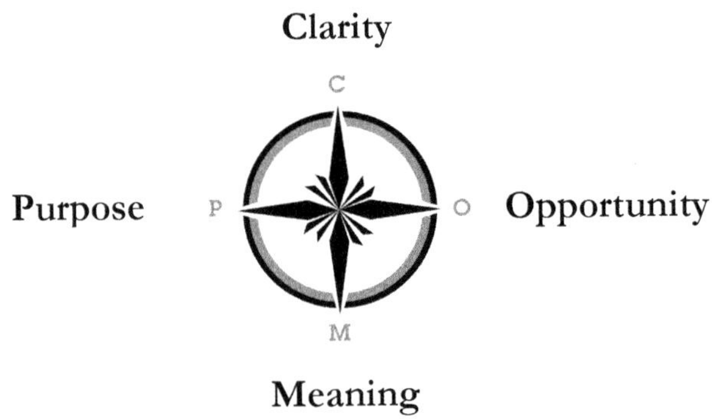

The New Possibilities for Baby Boomer Business Owners

When you think of a future in which you are no longer running your company, you may automatically assume that you are thinking about "retirement." But the old model known as "retirement" is inappropriate for Baby Boomers. Because of our unique history and accomplishments, Baby Boomers in their 50s and 60s are not ready to go "out to pasture" or sit on the porch in rocking chairs. Instead, we are getting ready to move into a new stage of active life, that can go on for another 10, 20 or 30 years. This realization opens up many new opportunities for what you personally could do in the next stage of your life.

This new perspective is especially important for Baby Boomer business owners. As a successful business owner, you have the experience, intelligence, health and wealth to do something new and exciting with the rest of your life. But in order to move into this rewarding new future, you need to discover what it is that you really want to do – and you need to transition successfully out of your company, so you are able to live your new dream.

Even though as a Baby Boomer business owner you have great new potentials available to you, you also face a unique challenge. There are many powerful reasons why you may <u>not</u> want to leave your company. These factors are so compelling that many owners don't even want to <u>think</u> about leaving.

Why Owners Don't Want to Think about Leaving

Here are some familiar feelings that I've heard many owners express when they think about the prospect of leaving their companies.

- Fear of an unknown future
- Owning and running your company gives your life meaning and purpose
- Leaving will lead to loss of social status
- Leaving will lead to loss of identity
- No vision of what to do in your new life
- Leaving feels like "a black hole"
- Thinking about leaving feels like "death"

Do these reactions sound familiar?

Do any of these reasons resonate with you? (See Figure 1-B.)

Figure 1-B

Many Owners Say That Thinking about Leaving Their Companies "Feels Like Falling into a Black Hole."

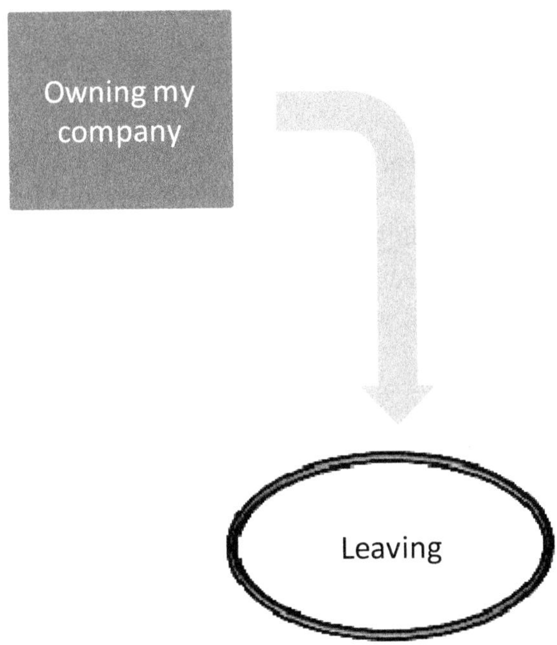

What is the "Transition Process?"

When business owners and their advisors talk about the "transition process," they are usually referring to the business transition – that is, the process of a business owner transferring the company to new ownership – for example, passing it on to family members or selling it to an outside buyer. Because financial and business transactions are central to this transfer, it is also referred to as the "transactional process."

I suggest that the transition process needs a more comprehensive and emotionally relevant definition. I talk about the "Transition Process" – capital "T," capital "P" – which includes the process of an owner:

1. Thinking about and planning a personally meaningful and fulfilling new life that you want to live;
2. Then thinking about your business transition goals, designing your business transition strategy and implementing this strategy by transferring your company to new ownership (the "transactional" part of the process);
3. And then moving into your meaningful and fulfilling new life.

This is STPI's definition of the "Transition Process".

The Transition Process Can Be Painful, but It Is Also Rewarding

Engaging in the Transition Process is a challenging experience. It requires that you make major changes in your life and step out into the unknown. Change is always difficult, stepping into the unknown can be scary and the entire process can bring up painful emotions.

However, the Transition Process can also bring many positive new outcomes and opportunities for you and your company.

- The Transition Process gives you the opportunity to do something new with your life. It opens up new possibilities and new sources of fulfillment for you.

- The Transition Process also gives your company the opportunity to change and grow. New ownership can bring new ideas and new ways of doing things into your company. And the process of preparing your company for new ownership can help you recognize and deal with its weaknesses and build on its strengths, improving operations and increasing the bottom line.

The Transition Process Is Both an Intellectual and an Emotional Process

As I have learned during 15 years of working with owners in transition, the process of leaving your company successfully and moving on to a fulfilling new life has four components. The Transition Process is:

A personal process
A business process
A financial process
An emotional process

As business owners, we're not used to talking about or considering our emotions when making business and financial decisions. However, an owner's personal experiences, relationships, values and emotions are central to the challenge of creating a successful business transition and moving on to a meaningful and fulfilling new life.

Business owners – and the professional advisors you use, such as your lawyer, accountant, etc. – are quite competent and comfortable when thinking about and working with business and financial issues.

But we're not accustomed to bringing our personal lives – our experiences, relationships and values from outside of work – into the process of thinking about and implementing our business and financial decisions.

And we're certainly not used to talking about or considering our emotions when making business and financial decisions!

However, an owner's personal experiences, relationships, values and emotions are central to the challenge of creating a successful business transition and moving on to a meaningful and fulfilling new life.

The system I created – Integrative Transition Planning – allows a business owner to feel comfortable thinking strategically about both the Head and Heart aspects of the Transition Process.

In order to help business owners transition successfully into exciting and fulfilling new futures, I created a methodology that allows them to take a businesslike approach to thinking strategically about not only business and financial issues, but also about their personal lives and emotions related to the Transition Process. In other words, the system I created allows the owner to feel comfortable thinking strategically about both the Head and Heart issues involved in the Transition Process.

The methodical, step-by-step system I developed is based on the experiences and familiar thinking styles of business owners. In addition to using facts, logic and sound business principles, this system also allows owners to bring key aspects of their personal lives into the Transition Process, and allows them to feel comfortable while becoming aware of and thinking strategically about their own emotions in relation to the Transition Process.

I call this unique approach "Integrative Transition Planning." I founded the Successful Transition Planning Institute (STPI) to educate Baby Boomer business owners about this new approach, and to train other professional advisors so they can use Integrative Transition Planning with the business owners they work with. (See Figure 1-C.)

Figure 1-C

Integrative Transition Planning:

Strategic Thinking about Both the Head and Heart Issues of Your Transition Process Creates a Successful New Future – for Your Company and for Yourself.

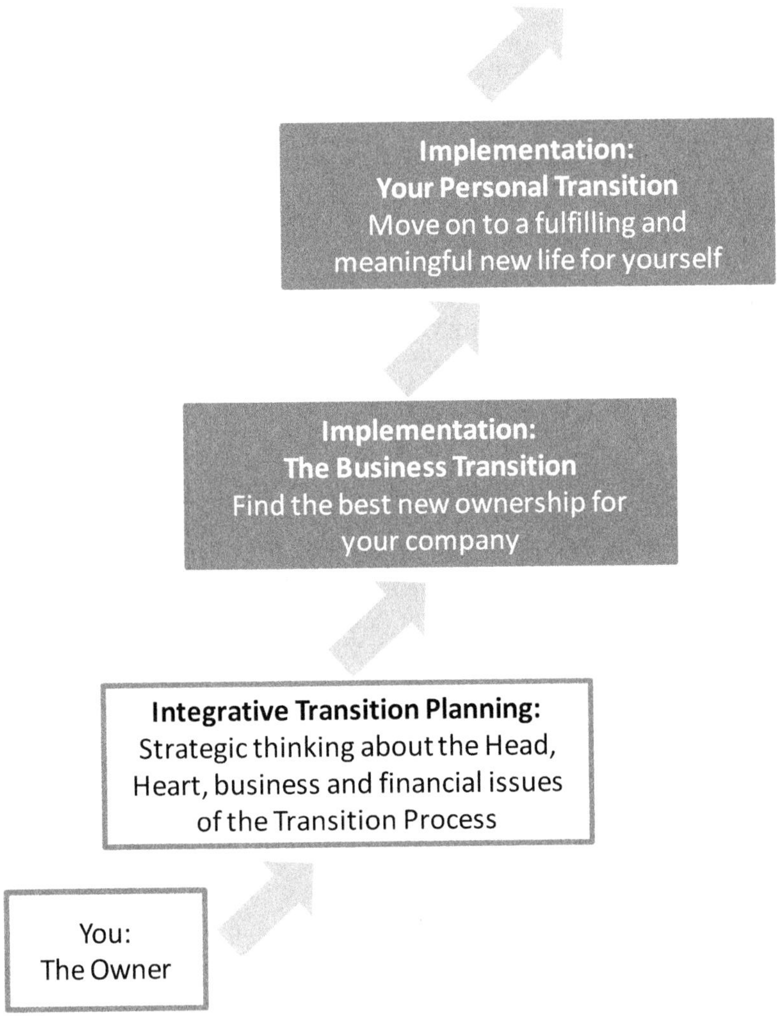

Thinking about Your Personal Future Comes First

Through working with many business owners going through transitions, I discovered that before you try to think about or plan for the business transition, you first need to think about your personal future and create your unique dream of a personally meaningful new life that you can't wait to live.

Your vision of an exciting new personal future then becomes a very specific, concrete goal that you are aiming for. This personal vision keeps you motivated during the rest of the business transition and implementation process. Part II explains more about why your first step in planning for your new future should be to create a comprehensive and detailed Personal Transition Plan, and describes some of the methods STPI has created to help you think strategically about your vision and plan for your new personal future.

Before you try to think about or plan for the business transition process, you first need to create your unique dream of a personally meaningful new life that you can't wait to live. This personal vision keeps you motivated during the business transition process.

Expanding Your Thinking about Your Business and Personal Futures

Since many owners are reluctant to even think about leaving their companies, this new paradigm of Integrative Transition Planning begins by helping you, the owner, expand your thinking so you can become emotionally ready to consider the possibility of passing your company on to new owners and moving on to a new stage of your life.

STPI's unique Head and Heart approach allows you to recognize, honor and feel good about what you have created and accomplished as owner of your company. This approach also helps you expand your thinking so you can think more clearly and broadly about new possibilities – both for your company and for yourself – and can feel more comfortable and self-confident in planning for the Transition Process.

Here are some exercises that STPI uses to help owners think strategically about their emotions and expand their thinking about their futures.

1. **Rewards of being an owner**

   Being an owner provides you with many rewards and benefits. There are financial rewards. There are emotional rewards, which include feelings of accomplishment and self-esteem, being in charge, being a leader, having a sense of meaning and purpose in your life, creativity and social status. Being an owner also brings you relationships – with your employees, customers, vendors, etc.

   Now think about the following questions:

   - What emotional rewards do you get from being an owner?
   - What other rewards or benefits do you get from being an owner?

2. **Honoring your legacy**
   - As the owner of your company, what have you created or accomplished that you are proud of?
   - What in your company would you like to see continued if you were to leave?

3. **Limitations of being an owner**
   - What has being an owner prevented you from doing?
   - What long-held dreams or new opportunities could you pursue, if you were able to transfer your company to new

owners and came away with the money you need for a fulfilling new life?

Did you enjoy thinking about these questions? Did they stimulate your thinking? Did they help you feel more appreciated for who you are and what you have accomplished? Did you get any new insights as a result of these questions?

This was just a taste of Integrative Transition Planning. The rest of this book describes many other important insights that my colleagues and I have learned as a result of working with owners in transition, and presents other questions and exercises that STPI has developed and that professional advisors associated with STPI use, to help Baby Boomer business owners create successful new futures for their companies and themselves.

Taking Time to Focus on Yourself

Many owners feel that they don't have time to think about their futures. However, one of the most important gifts you can give yourself is taking the time, now, to reflect more deeply on what is truly meaningful to you, to explore new possibilities about who you can be and what you can do in the next stage of your life.

Taking the time to read this book can start you in this direction. As a Baby Boomer business owner, you are now facing the challenge of having to think about transitioning your business and moving on with your life. There is no better time than now to step back, reflect on your past accomplishments, then expand your thinking so you can create a new future for your company and a meaningful and exciting new life for yourself.

CHAPTER 2

Fifteen Ways to Leave Your Company Unsuccessfully – and How to Avoid Them

1. Carl F. was the owner of a firm that manufactured consumer electronic products. When he began thinking about the possibility of leaving his company, he would swing from one emotional extreme to the other. Sometimes he felt that he could not wait to leave his firm; other times, he woke up in a cold sweat, caused by the very idea of leaving his business. He continually distracted himself from the larger question of "What should I do with my company?" by focusing exclusively on his daily "to-do" list. He was never able to take the next step to begin the process of actively transitioning out of his company, and he is still there.

2. Allen G. owned a company that manufactured promotional products for other businesses and organizations. He thought he wanted to sell his company, but wasn't really sure. Constantly going back and forth thinking about what to do with his company diverted his time and attention away from running the business. Allen eventually contacted a CPA who began to do the necessary work to help sell the company. Then the CPA got a phone call from Allen, saying that he had changed his mind and no longer wanted to sell.

   As a result of being unsure about their futures, Allen's employees became demoralized, which resulted in reduced productivity and lower profits for the company. Also, Allen's decision not to sell his company after it had been listed reduced its value and led to reduced sales revenue, since the customers became unsure whether the company would remain open.

   A year and a half later, Allen again decided that he wanted to sell the company. But this time, having been burned once, his CPA did not put a lot of effort into helping him sell it. Other business intermediaries that Allen went to were also reluctant to spend their time and energy trying to sell his company, because Allen had pulled it off the market once before for no apparent reason. Allen never sold his company, and he is still running it.

3. Philip H. was a high-tech manufacturer who had built his business over the past 20 years into a company with annual sales revenue of $17 million. Deciding that it was time for him to sell, Philip went to an M&A firm and paid them a retainer to sell the company for him. The M&A firm found a buyer, they were three-quarters into the transaction, and Philip was saying all the right things at the conference table. Suddenly Philip got "cold feet" and killed the deal for no apparent business reason.

4. Karen J., in her sixties, had built a successful retail business over many years and was highly respected in her industry. She hoped that her son, who had occasionally worked at the company, would take over the business when she left. Meanwhile, her son had begun attending a prestigious business school. When Karen asked him when he might be ready to join her company full-time, he was non-committal. He was meeting some really exciting professors and other business owners through his school, and Mom's business was no longer appealing to him. With her son out of the picture, Karen didn't have a "Plan B" for a successor.

5. George K., co-owner of a successful real estate business in New York City, was raising his family in an exclusive suburban community near the city. His kids went to excellent schools, his youngest to a prestigious school in Boston. Then George died suddenly. It took two years to settle his estate because he had not planned well with his partners. Because of his poor planning and denial of his

own mortality, the business floundered, his wife had to get a job quickly and their daughter had to leave her prominent school.

6. Tom L. was a builder who spent 30 years growing his business. In his sixties he sold his share of the company to his younger partners for a good financial settlement. To fill his time, Tom now spends his days doing chores and making things in his workshop in the garage (his wife doesn't let him smoke in the house), but this does not make him happy. He ponders what else he could be doing, but can't find any answers. He feels completely alone.

7. Robert M., who owned a medical device supply company, successfully sold his business to a larger company in the same field. Robert was used to spending 60 to 70 hours a week at work. After selling his company he moved to a small town in the southern U.S. where he hoped to find new work as a consultant, but was unable to find clients. Robert now had too much time on his hands, and he began doing things for the sake of "killing time." One morning he woke up and realized that his new life was meaningless. Even though he was constantly busy, his activities didn't give him a sense of purpose. Robert felt like a gerbil in a cage – running all day and going nowhere.

8. Gordon N.'s company manufactured small parts for computers. He decided to retire, sold his company to his management team, and moved to a new community where

he could play golf all day. He soon came to the realization that playing golf day in and day out was no longer fun, but didn't know what else to do. Now when Gordon wakes up each morning, he has nothing to look forward to during the day. Not only is he bored and depressed; he has also become overweight and developed heart disease and diabetes.

9. Warren P., who lived in New England, sold his electronic parts manufacturing company to another small company. His plan for retirement was for his wife and him to uproot their lives from the community where they had lived for many years, and move all the way across the U.S. to a suburb outside of Houston, Texas where they could spend time with their grandkids. A short time after Warren and his wife moved to a condo near their son's home, they discovered that their grandchildren did not want to spend all day sitting on Grandpa's lap. They had soccer games to go to and other friends who they wanted to be with. Since Warren's one plan for what he was going to do after he retired wasn't working, and he had no other ideas of what he wanted to do, he became increasingly unhappy. He also developed unexplained pain, high blood pressure and ulcers, which had never been a problem for him while he was working.

In these case studies, the names and other identifying information have been changed to respect privacy.

During our many years working with business owners, my colleagues and I at STPI have seen how difficult it can be for owners to leave their companies successfully.

Many owners simply refuse to think about the possibility of leaving. Lacking any alternatives, these owners may end up "dying at their desks." Or unexpected circumstances may force them to leave involuntarily. With no plan for either their own futures or the future of their companies, their personal lives become diminished, and their unexpected departures can harm the well-being of both their companies and their families.

We've also seen owners who realized that it was time to move on, but didn't know what was involved in creating a successful transition. These owners may have had a very limited "plan" for passing on their companies, that didn't work out. Or the transition process may have left them emotionally or financially unsatisfied, or both.

We've met owners who thought they wanted to leave, and who actually began the transition process by paying a retainer to an M&A firm to help them find a buyer for their company – then in the middle of the search, these owners suddenly got "cold feet," told the M&A firm they'd changed their minds and didn't really want to sell.

In fact, this experience of an owner suddenly changing his mind about leaving has happened so often that it has a name; it's called "Seller's Remorse." And because so many M&A firms have been burned over the years by owners who suddenly experienced Seller's Remorse and unexpectedly backed out of the deal, many M&A firms are now charging a penalty to owners who change their minds about selling – in addition to keeping the owner's retainer.

There are a variety of reasons why business owners fail to transition successfully. Some of these reasons are intellectual – the owners' lack of experience about how to transition themselves and their companies successfully. Other reasons are emotional –caused by the owners' fears about leaving, which makes it difficult for them to think clearly about their future or prevents them from even wanting to think about it. For most owners, the obstacles to a successful transition are both intellectual and emotional.

What is a successful transition? Here is the definition that my colleagues and I at STPI use (see Figure 2-A).

Figure 2-A

Defining a Successful Transition

Leaving your company successfully means that:

1. You have a plan now for the new life you want to live.

2. You leave your company so that:
    a. You come away with the money you need for your new life.
    b. Your company continues successfully after you have left.
    c. You are able to live the new life you have designed.

How does the definition of a successful transition in Figure 2-A sound to you?

Is this a goal that you would like to aim for?

Even though transitioning successfully may sound like a desirable goal, my colleagues and I have identified at least 15 different ways through which an owner can fail to achieve it. We believe that an important part of helping owners transition successfully is by letting you become aware of potential pitfalls in the Transition Process, so you can recognize, prepare for and avoid them.

Also, as you learn about these unsuccessful ways to leave your company, you can recognize other owners who failed to transition successfully and understand why they failed. Being able to put a name to each of these possible pitfalls can help you gain more clarity, think more strategically, and plan for and implement your own Transition Process more successfully.

A. <u>Not leaving</u>

1. **An R&D approach (repression and denial)**
   Owners don't even want to think about leaving, so they don't plan ahead. They do nothing. Doing nothing makes owners and their companies vulnerable when unexpected events occur, and can lead to business decline, financial loss or to personal and family upheaval.

B. <u>Leaving involuntarily</u>

2. **Unexpected illness or disability**

If an owner has to leave suddenly due to unexpected illness or disability, but has made no plans for the future of the company, then the owner, their family and business can all suffer.

3. **Sudden death ("Dying at your desk")**
   If an owner has made no plans for the future of the company and dies suddenly, their family and business can both suffer.

C. **<u>Trying to leave (but being unsuccessful at it)</u>**

4. **Making an impulsive decision**
   When owners suddenly decide they want to leave their companies, but don't take time to prepare or plan. Making an impulsive decision often happens when some negative event occurs – for example, the business is doing badly, or the owner unexpectedly develops a medical condition and suddenly has to think about leaving. But suddenly deciding to leave your business, or quickly trying to pass it on to someone else doesn't give you time to explore all your options. You can't make the best decisions, and you probably won't be able to get the money you want for your company.

5. **Owner's Indecision**
   Owner's Indecision refers to owners who think that maybe they want to sell their companies, but they're really not sure. They might go to an M&A firm, investment banker or other business intermediary and say "I'm interested in selling my company." But very soon the owner goes back to the intermediary and says, "I changed my mind. I don't really want to sell," and take the company off the market. In fact, the owners are really only "kicking the tires" or "just looking." They are not serious sellers.

Many business intermediaries have been burned by Owner's Indecision. Because of this, owners who change their minds can develop a bad reputation, and may not be able to find an intermediary willing to work with them when they really are ready to transition out of their companies.

6. Seller's Remorse

Seller's Remorse is, unfortunately, a very familiar scenario. An owner decides they want to sell their company and goes to a business intermediary to help them find a buyer. The negotiations may actually have begun – and all of a sudden the owner gets "cold feet." The owner wasn't emotionally ready to sell, and stops the deal.

The owner who feels Seller's Remorse may lose more than the retainer they paid to the intermediary. Because so many business intermediaries have been "burned" by owners who suddenly backed out of a deal, firms are now charging penalties to owners who get Seller's Remorse and pull out of the selling process. The owner may also get a bad reputation and be unable to find an intermediary willing to work with them when they really are ready to transition out of their company.

D. <u>Trying to transfer the company to new ownership (but doing it unsuccessfully)</u>

7. Making a limited or incorrect decision

In this scenario, the owner has a fixed idea of what they want to do with their company (for example, "I want to leave it to my son.") But this may be the wrong choice. It may be the wrong person, or the person selected may not be ready to take over. Or the company may fail later because it was passed on to the wrong person, which can be problematic for the former owner (and their family) if they were depending on future income from the company to support their new lives.

Owners need to be aware of and compare all their options before making a decision about who the best new owner would be.

8. **Trying to do it all-by-myself**
   This refers to an owner who is trying to personally sell the company to new owners, and at the same time trying to keep the company running successfully day-to-day. The owner lacks the expertise to find a new owner, doesn't have enough time and energy to focus attention on both goals at once, and may fail at both. This owner needs to work with a team of professionals experienced in the transition process, who can help the owner create and implement their transition plan.

9. **Working with conflicting advisors**
   This owner seeks the advice and support of professionals experienced in the transition process, but the different advisors give the owner different advice. The owner becomes confused and frustrated, and may stop the transition process. (The owner should have assembled a team of transition advisors, who will work collaboratively to help the owner transition successfully.)

10. **Inadequate value**
    Because owners didn't plan adequately, didn't improve the value of their companies or didn't work with advisors experienced in the transition process, they didn't get as much money for their companies as they could have.

E. Retiring Unsuccessfully

11. Exit-decision remorse

In this scenario, an owner makes a quick decision that they want to leave their company and they quickly transfer their company to new owners. They don't take the time to look at all their options, and don't have a clear idea of what they want to do with their life after leaving their company. After they have left, they begin to have second thoughts: "Did I make the correct decision? Maybe I should have stayed working longer. Maybe I should have tried to get more money for my company," etc. Instead of enjoying their new life, they are continually obsessed by the thought that they made the wrong decision.

12. Retirement remorse

Owners may successfully transfer their companies to new ownership, but if they didn't have a plan for a fulfilling new future, they don't know what to do now with all their free time. They can become bored, even depressed, and miss their old lives as owners, because at least then they had something interesting and meaningful to do. They think, "I shouldn't have left. I don't know what to do with my life now."

13. Retirement rut

In this scenario, owners have successfully left their companies but didn't plan what to do with their new lives. Because as owners they were busy all the time, they now find ways to become constantly busy, but these new activities don't give them a sense of meaning or purpose. They have dug themselves into a hole of meaningless activity and feel unsatisfied and depressed, but don't know how to make their lives more meaningful.

14. Post-Transaction Stress Disorder (PTSD)

In Post-Transaction Stress Disorder, owners successfully left their companies, and even had a plan for what to do with their new lives. But their plan was very limited and one-dimensional – for example, "I'll play golf," or "I'll spend time with my grandkids." They soon realize that their one plan is not working out as they imagined, and this one activity isn't enough to bring them new meaning and purpose. They become bored and depressed. What they needed was a more multi-sided, comprehensive and well thought-out plan for their new lives.

15. Financial deficit

Financial deficit occurs when owners leave their companies and discover too late that they don't have enough money to live fulfilling, successful new lives. Financial deficit can occur for several reasons, including lack of planning; getting inadequate value for the business; or making a wrong choice in new owners, who were supposed to provide the former owner with future income, but who couldn't run the business well, so it failed and the owner didn't continue to receive the expected future income.

How to leave your company unsuccessfully

Here are some problems that can prevent an owner from creating a successful Transition Plan:

1. Lack of information about what to expect and about your options

2. Unresolved emotions and fears about leaving your company

3. Limited thinking about your future possibilities

4. Lack of a clear vision for your future

5. Lack of clear goals for your personal and business futures

6. Lack of a plan for how to achieve your goals

7. Lack of support from professional advisors experienced in the Transition Process

The rest of this book explains how you can respond to each of these problems, so you can create a successful transition for your company and yourself.

CHAPTER 3

The Head and Heart of an Owner: A Strategic Approach to Creating a New Future for Your Business and Yourself

Integrative Transition Planning provides a wholistic approach for creating your new future. In order to transition out of your company successfully and create a meaningful new future for yourself, you need to think strategically about your new goals and plans – personal, business and financial. You also need to be aware of and work strategically with the emotions that can arise when you think about your life as an owner and consider the prospect of leaving.

STPI calls this double challenge "the Head and Heart issues of the Transition Process." To put it another way, "the Transition Process is both an intellectual and an emotional process."

The Emotional Side of the Transition Process

How your emotions affect your ability to think about a new future

Why are we talking about emotions, anyway? Why is the Transition Process an emotional process?

As a business owner, you have deep emotional ties to your company and to your identity as an owner. The thought of leaving naturally brings up many strong emotional reactions.

Being an owner gives meaning and purpose to your life. It gives you a sense of identity and provides you with social status and respect from your community. You are good at being an owner, and you have probably not spent much time or energy thinking about what you might do instead that could bring you the same feelings of self-esteem, accomplishment and fulfillment.

As an owner, you also have deep emotional ties to your company itself. The company is your "baby." It was your hard work that built it successfully, and it will be difficult to let it go. Running your company also brings you many rewarding relationships – with employees, customers, vendors and other professional colleagues.

How can you replace the rewards of being an owner? How can you replace what your company means to you? It's not easy. When you try to think about your future after leaving, you may come up empty. Or thinking about leaving may bring up feelings of uneasiness and dread.

What makes this more complicated is the fact that as business owners, we are not accustomed to talking or thinking about our emotions, especially not in our work. As owners, we are supposed to deal with numbers and hard facts.

However, the many examples we've been describing of owners who left unsuccessfully show how your emotions and fears can sabotage your attempts at leaving. Your painful emotions and fears about leaving can put you under stress, which can be bad for your health. These emotions can be especially insidious if you are not even aware that you are feeling them. And your painful emotions and fears – whether recognized or unrecognized – can prevent you from being able to think clearly and strategically about your future.

Your unrecognized emotions and fears can sabotage your attempts at leaving, and can prevent you from being able to think clearly and strategically about your future.

That's why the Transition Process is an emotional process. And that's why, in addition to providing you with the intellectual information you need, STPI's new paradigm of Integrative Transition Planning also includes:

- helping you become aware of your emotions and fears related to the prospect of leaving your company;
- showing you how to transform your transition-related fears and limiting emotions, so they will not sabotage or block you;
- and showing you how to create new sources of identity, self-esteem, meaning and purpose for your new life.

The Intellectual Side of the Transition Process

Thinking strategically about your new future so you can achieve your transition goals

As an owner contemplating the prospect of transferring your company to new ownership and moving on to a meaningful new life, you want to leave your company successfully. Recall how we defined a successful transition:

Leaving your company successfully means that:

1. **You have a plan now for the new life you want to live.**
2. **You leave your company so that:**

    a. **You come away with the money you need for your new life.**
    b. **Your company continues successfully after you have left.**
    c. **You are able to live the new life you have designed.**

Being able to leave your company successfully according to this definition requires that:

- You take time to think about the personal, business and financial goals you want to accomplish through the Transition Process; and

- You know what to expect during the business transition process, so you can be prepared for what is going to happen and can effectively achieve both your personal and business transition goals.

Here are some questions to ask yourself as you think about creating your transition goals.

Personal goals

- Am I mentally and emotionally ready to think about leaving my company?
- Am I mentally and emotionally ready to create a clear and comprehensive plan for my new life?
- Can I create a plan for my new life that will fill my new future with meaning and purpose?

Business goals

- What changes do I need to make to my company, so it can continue successfully without me?
- Who would be the best new owner(s) for my company?
- What legacy would I like to see carried on in the company after I have left?

Financial goals

- How much money will I need for my new life?
- Will I need money from my company to support my new life?
- How much money will I need from my company, and when will I need it?

These questions are only a small sample of the issues involved in creating your transition goals. Part II of this book describes more fully how to create your <u>personal</u> transition goals, including your personal financial goals. Part III explains what is involved in creating your <u>business</u> transition goals, including your business-related financial goals, and describes what you can expect during the business transition process so you will be prepared for this process and can more effectively achieve your business, personal and financial transition goals.

Determining Your Mental and Emotional Readiness for Transition Planning

Are you ready to begin thinking successfully about your own Transition Process? To find out, try answering each of the following questions.

- Have you thought about leaving your company?
- Do you have any plans for how you will leave your company?
- Do you have any thoughts or plans for what you will do with your company and who its new owner(s) might be?
- Do you have any thoughts or plans for what you want to do with your life after you've left your company?
- How do these questions make you feel?

Even though most of these questions can be answered with facts and figures, they probably also stir up emotional reactions in you. This is just one example of how the intellectual and emotional aspects of the Transition Process are so deeply intertwined.

Creating a Strategic Transition Plan That Includes Both the Head and Heart Aspects of the Transition Process

One of the most important parts of achieving a successful Transition Process is creating a detailed, written strategic Transition Plan for your personal and business futures.

You've probably learned from your own business experience that when a problem arises, the best approach is for you (or you and your staff) to think about the problem strategically, create a clear strategy, and even better, develop a written strategic plan for responding to the problem.

Having a clear vision and plan for what you want to accomplish makes it much more likely that you will achieve your goals. If you don't know where you want to go, you're not going anywhere. And this is true not only in business, but in all of life.

If you don't know where you want to go, you're not going anywhere. This is true not only in business, but in all of life. Having a clear vision and plan for what you want to achieve through the Transition Process – and putting that vision into a written strategic plan – is essential for achieving your personal and business transition goals.

Because the Transition Process involves so many different issues, you need to take time to think strategically about both the goals you want to achieve, and how you can achieve them most effectively. Then you need to create a detailed, written strategic plan that lays out your personal, business, and financial goals and your strategic plans for how you will achieve those goals.

You don't have to do all this by yourself. Successful owners work with a team of professional advisors experienced in the Transition Process, who can help you create and implement your strategic plans. A detailed strategic plan, written down so you can regularly refer to it, is essential to help you transition successfully.

Why You Need to Plan

Owners who don't plan will fail to get what they need from the Transition Process. The facts bear this out. In a recent survey of business owners who sold their companies, 75% of these former owners reported that they regretted having sold their businesses, because it did not accomplish their personal and business objectives. (www.evolvebusinessgroup.com)

Why did these former owners fail to achieve their objectives? The owners surveyed admitted that they:

- Did not make well thought-out exit decisions.
- Were not aware of all their options.
- Had not developed a plan for their lives after leaving their companies.
- Did not know professionals experienced in transition planning, who could have helped them create a successful transition strategy.

Other surveys document that most Baby Boomer business owners have not yet begun transition planning. Here are the startling facts:

- Many business owners have as much as 90% of their wealth tied up in their companies. (www.evolvebusinessgroup.com)
- 70 % of Baby Boomer business owners do not have plans for how they will leave their companies. (www.evolvebusinessgroup.com)
- 60 % of business owners between the ages of 55-64 have not discussed their plans for leaving their companies with their business partners or spouses. (www.rocg.com)

And here are some of the reasons owners report for why they have not yet begun to do transition planning:

- Owners don't want to think about leaving.
- They think it's too early to plan.
- They don't have time to spend on planning.
- They fear that the transition process will be too complicated.
- They don't know experienced advisors who can help them plan for and implement the transition process.
  (These responses come from STPI's discussions with owners.)

It's because of responses like those above that I founded STPI and created the new paradigm of Integrative Transition Planning. Since STPI's system helps the owner deal with both the Head and Heart aspects of transition planning, it is specifically designed to help you successfully create and achieve both your personal and business goals in a way that brings you not only financial success but also new personal meaning.

Two Types of Transitions Require Planning

STPI's unique approach recognizes that in an owner's Transition Process, two distinct types of transitions are actually taking place – your personal transition and your business transition.

Your personal transition. This transition is about your life and your identity. It is a transition from owning and running your company, to moving into the next stage of your life, with new activities, new relationships with your spouse and family, and new sources of identity, meaning and fulfillment.

Your business transition. This is a transition for both you and your company. It is a transition from a company owned and run by you, to a company with new ownership. This transition may include new goals for your company, improvements in your company's operations, and new organizational structure in order to allow the company to continue successfully when you are no longer running it.

In order to achieve a successful Transition Process, you need to create two distinct plans – your Business Transition Plan and your Personal Transition Plan.

Because you will be engaged in two distinct transitions, this means that in order to achieve a successful Transition Process, you need to think strategically about both your personal transition and your business transition. And you need to create two distinct plans – your Business Transition Plan and your Personal Transition Plan.

Your Business Transition Plan includes your business transition goals and how you will achieve them. Through creating your Business Transition Plan you:

- Become aware of all your options for new ownership, so you can decide on the best new ownership for your company.
- Plan how to prepare your company for the Transition Process.
- Plan how to achieve your desired financial outcomes when transferring your company to new ownership.

Your Personal Transition Plan includes your personal transition goals and how you will achieve them. Through creating your Personal Transition Plan you:

- Create a clear vision of your personal future and a successful strategy for making it happen.
- Plan for how you will achieve personal and emotional satisfaction in your new life.
- Can feel peace of mind about moving on to a new life.

Taking Time to Plan

It takes time to do successful transition planning. It takes time to think about your personal and business transition goals and create strategic step-by-step plans for their implementation. It requires time to reflect on what you really want to do in your new life, and time to collect the information you will need to create your goals and develop your strategies for a successful personal and business transition.

It also takes time to implement your plans. A typical business transition can take between 2 to 5 years. This includes:

- Preparing your personal and business goals and strategic plans.
- Implementing your Business Transition Plan and transferring your company to new owners through a deal that best meets your goals.
- Working with your transition advisors to design, implement and refine your transition strategies.

And that's why it's not "too early to plan." Planning for the next stage of your life and for a new future for your company are two of the most important activities you can do right now. That's why now is the time to begin your transition planning.

You Are Not Alone: Working with Transition Advisors

As a successful business owner, you already rely on a team of professional advisors, such as a CPA and a business attorney, to help you with your business. Your professional advisors provide information, analysis and other types of expertise that you personally do not have or that you do not want to be bothered with. You have other activities you need to focus on so you can run your company effectively.

You also rely on a team of professional advisors for your personal life, such as a personal attorney, a personal financial planner or wealth management professional, perhaps an estate planning attorney. You know that you can't manage all the aspects of either your personal financial life or your business by yourself, and you want the best possible professional advice and support.

The same considerations also apply to the Transition Process. Successful transition planning is a multidisciplinary endeavor. Even though as a business owner you have considerable experience and expertise in how to run a successful business, you probably have little or no experience in how to successfully transition out of your company and how to transfer it to the best new owners.

> **You already rely on a team of professional advisors to help you with your business and personal life. You can't manage all the aspects of your business or your personal finances by yourself, and you want the best possible professional advice and support. The same considerations apply to the Transition Process. No single individual has all the knowledge and expertise to design and implement a successful transition plan. Successful owners work with a Collaborative Team of Transition Advisors to help them design and implement their successful transition strategies.**

Furthermore, as Chapter 2 noted, an owner who tries to "do it all-by-myself" will be torn between trying to run the company successfully, and simultaneously trying to find new owners and transferring the company on the most advantageous terms. Trying to run your company successfully and transition it successfully at the same time – especially when you don't have the needed transition expertise – means that you will probably do neither activity well.

Just as running a business requires many different types of professional expertise, successful transition planning also requires many types of professional support. No single individual has all the knowledge, information or expertise needed.

Owners, along with their professional advisors – both current advisors, and additional new advisors experienced in the Transition Process – all need to participate in the process of designing and implementing the owners' Personal and Business Transition Plans.

A Transition Planning Consultant trained by STPI can help you with the Head and Heart issues of Integrative Transition Planning – becoming mentally and emotionally ready for the Transition Process, thinking about your Personal and Business Transition Goals, and designing a unique comprehensive plan for a new life you can't wait to live. (See Chapter 12.)

In addition to your lawyer, CPA, personal financial planner and a Transition Planning Consultant, other professional advisors who can help you with the Transition Process may also include a management consultant, M&A specialist and other types of professionals who can help you design and implement various aspects of your transition plans. Advisors can help you determine the value of your business, help you improve your company's operations so it will be successful after you have left, and can help you find/negotiate with new owners. (Part III explains more about how professional advisors can help you create a successful Transition Process.)

Figure 3-A presents a visual image that STPI uses to represent the ways in which different types of transition advisors participate to help you create a successful Transition Process. This image shows four key outcomes: Make it matter, Make it better, Make it happen, Make it last.

Make it matter: Make your transition planning process more enjoyable and satisfying. This is what an STPI-trained Transition Planning Consultant does. (See Chapter 12.)

Make it better: Make your business more valuable to new owners. Various professional advisors can help you achieve this outcome, depending on your specific situation.

Make it happen: Ensure that your company is transferred successfully to new ownership. Your situation will determine the advisors who can help you achieve this outcome.

Make it last: Ensure that your new wealth which you get from transferring your company to new ownership will last as long as you need it. Various professional advisors can help you achieve this outcome. (See Chapter 11.)

Figure 3-A

Four Key Outcomes That Professional Transition Advisors Can Help You Achieve for a Successful Personal and Business Transition Process

Make it better

Make it happen

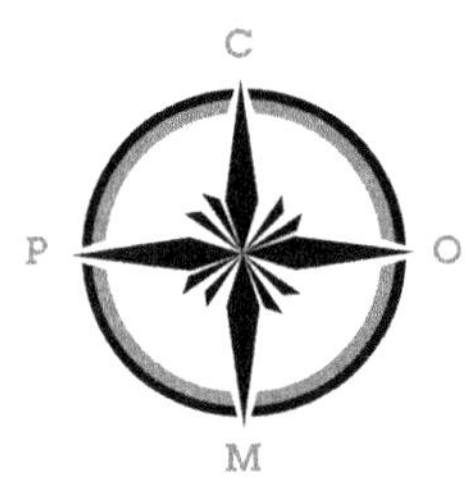

Make it matter

Make it last

One problem that can prevent a successful transition is when the owner tries to work with all these transition advisors separately. Individual advisors may offer conflicting advice, causing the owner to become confused and discouraged about the transition process.

The solution to this problem is to work with a Collaborative Team of Transition Advisors. You can either assemble your own collaborative team, or look for an already-established team of transition advisors who regularly work together. (Chapter 11 explains how to find and work with a Collaborative Team of Transition Advisors.)

Other participants who can also make valuable contributions to your Transition Process include your employees, as well as your spouse and other family members.

All the people mentioned above can help – by encouraging you to reflect on what you truly want from the Transition Process, providing needed information or analysis and assisting with or actually carrying out parts of the planning and implementation process, based on their specific knowledge and expertise.

Exit Planning and Transition Planning, Transactional Advisors and Transition Advisors

Advisors who help an owner transition often refer to what they do as "exit planning." Exit planning focuses on the technical, business and financial aspects of how you will leave your company and what you intend to do with your company. This is also known as the "transactional part" of the exit process, and the advisors who work in this area are often referred to as "transactional advisors."

Transactional advisors are professional advisors skilled in the nuts and bolts of the transition process. They include the advisors who do financial and tax planning, who determine the value of your company, advise you on how to prepare your company for transition and find and negotiate with the new owners to help you get the best deal.

Transactional advisors are skilled at what they do and are an essential part of the Transition Process. But there's more to the Transition Process than just the business and financial transactions.

Many transactional (nuts-and-bolts) advisors are now recognizing that they need to collaborate with other kinds of transition advisors, who help the owner first become mentally and emotionally ready to engage in transition planning and implementation. Too many transactional advisors have been burned by owners who thought they wanted to sell their companies, but then got "cold feet" and suddenly pulled out of the transaction process because they were not emotionally ready to leave their companies.

That's why my colleagues and I at STPI use the term "transition planning" to refer to the overall process. This emphasizes the fact that in order to leave your company successfully, you are making a transition not only out of your company, but into a fulfilling new life. Calling this process transition planning (rather than exit planning) is both technically more comprehensive and accurate, and also offers a more emotionally encouraging view of the new future that you, the owner, are aiming for.

And that's why STPI trains professional advisors to deal with both the Head and Heart aspects of the Transition Process. The Transition Planning Consultants associated with STPI work with owners to help them become mentally and emotionally ready to think clearly about and be willing to engage fully in the Transition Process. Owners who are mentally and emotionally ready to engage in the Transition Process can then work successfully with transactional advisors to achieve their successful business and personal transitions.

FINDING YOUR NEW OWNER

PART II

HOW TO CREATE A NEW FUTURE YOU CAN'T WAIT TO LIVE

CHAPTER 4

From Being CEO of Your Company to Becoming CEO of Your Life

As a Baby Boomer business owner, you will soon be facing the challenge of having to transition into a new stage of your life. Going through this work-life transition can be uncomfortable, even scary. Here are some familiar responses that many owners share about this transition:

- Fear about an unknown future
- Fear about loss of identity
- Financial uncertainty
- Fear of aging
- Fear of losing your life's meaning and purpose

You can avoid thinking about this coming transition altogether. You may deal with it unsuccessfully because you are not aware of all the issues, decisions, choices and opportunities involved in this transition. Or you can prepare yourself for a successful business and personal transition by thinking strategically about both your emotions and the business and financial issues involved, and learning how to expand your thinking about the Transition Process.

Becoming the CEO of Your New Life

Right now you are the CEO of your company. In order to move successfully into a new future when you are no longer running your company, you have to become the "CEO of your new life."

The job of a CEO is to think big – to think about the Big Picture and make long-term plans for the future success of your company. In many ways, becoming CEO of your new life requires these same abilities. You have to think about the Big Picture of your own life and make long-term plans for your future personal success.

At the same time, thinking like a CEO about your personal future also requires some shifts in approach.

You also have to learn how to expand your thinking so that you are able to think strategically not only about the facts, but also about your emotions related to this transition.

And you have to think strategically not only about external issues such as your business and finances. You also need to think introspectively – looking within to discover what is truly important to you and what you really want to do in your new life.

Expanding Your Thinking about Your Future

You already know how to make strategic decisions for your company, but in the business world our decisions are often based on limited ways of thinking. In the work-world, we think competitively and externally. We compare ourselves against our competitors and measure our success based on external criteria such as goods sold and the financial bottom line. Our decisions are based on an "either/or" style of thinking.

But in planning for the next stage of your life you are not competing against anyone else. Instead, you need to look within and get answers from inside yourself, because your answers can only come from within. In planning for a successful new life, "success" will be measured not only by how much money you have made, but perhaps even more important, by how you are going to feel about your new life.

In order to plan effectively for your new future, you need to use "Transition Thinking." Transition Thinking is a dynamic way of thinking that allows you to think more broadly and deeply about both your personal future and the future of your company.

In order to plan effectively for your new future, you need to use "Transition Thinking." Transition Thinking is a dynamic way of thinking that allows you to think more broadly and deeply about both your personal future and the future of your company.

The rest of this chapter, and also the next chapter will show you how to expand your thinking about who you are, and discover the many new opportunities that can be available to you in your new life. Part III of this book shows you how to use Transition Thinking in thinking about and planning for the future of your business.

Expanding Your Thinking: Learning from Your Earlier Life-Transitions

You've already gone through many types of transitions in your life. To successfully think about and plan for the next transition you are facing, it will be helpful to think about earlier life-transitions you've gone through and reflect on what you learned from them.

A person goes through 10-20 major transitions in a lifetime. Here are some examples of major life-transitions that most of us go through:

- From childhood to adolescence
- From school to the work-world
- Moving out of your parents' home
- From youthful exploration to "settling down"
- Marriage
- Parenthood

These are just some familiar examples. There are many other types of life-transitions that people go through, or that you, yourself, may have gone through. And there are more transitions still to come.

Each time you go through a life-transition you change, learn and grow.

What life-transitions have <u>you</u> gone through?
What did you learn from them?

You can answer these two questions by using STPI's "Life-Transitions Exercise." To do this, take a piece of paper and divide it into four columns. Label the four columns "Transition Event," "Age," "Year It Happened" and "Lessons Learned."

Now think about your own earlier life-transitions. In the column for "Transition Event," list each of the life-transitions that you can think of (for example, "Went to college," "Got a job," "Moved away from home," etc.). You can either start from your earliest transitions and work forward to the present time, or you can start from the present and work backward in time to your younger years.

For each event, also fill in the age or year when it happened, and what lesson you learned through that specific life-transition.

When you have written down as many of your life-transitions as you can think of and the lesson you learned from each one, take some time to look over and reflect on your entire list. Now answer these two questions:

> What overall lessons have I learned from my life-transitions?
>
> How can I apply what I've learned to this new challenge of thinking about and preparing for transitioning out of my company and moving on to a new life?

Expanding Your Thinking: A Question of Identity

A central aspect of the work-life transition you are now facing is the challenge of creating a new identity for yourself.

Being owner of your business gives you a strong and rewarding sense of identity and a position of prestige and respect in your community. But because you've devoted so much of your time and energy to your role as owner of your company, you may have no idea of who you would be, or why you would be worthy of respect, if you were no longer running your company.

In order to think of yourself not as a business owner, but in your new life, an identity-shift needs to take place. It requires self-confidence and a strong sense of who you really are, to think about what you really want to do in the next stage of your life.

In order to think of yourself not as a business owner, but in your new life, an identity-shift needs to take place. It requires self-confidence and a strong sense of who you really are, to think about what you really want to do in the next stage of your life.

STPI's "Identity Exercise," will help you develop and move into this new sense of identity.

> To do the Identity Exercise, take another piece of paper and at the top of it write the words "Outside of My Work…"

Now go to Figure 4-A. For each of the questions in Figure 4-A, write down on your paper as many answers as you can think of. Try to give more than one answer to each question, if possible. Keep asking yourself – "And what else? And what else?"

If you are having difficulty answering these questions, think about <u>other</u> aspects of your life, <u>not</u> your activities as owner of your company. For example, think about:

> What you enjoyed doing when you were younger

> Your family life

Leisure activities you enjoy, such as a hobby or creative activity outside of work

Your participation in social groups not connected to the workplace – for example, in your neighborhood, in a social, community, or charitable organization or religious congregation

These may help you answer the questions in Figure 4-A.

Was it easy for you to answer the questions in Figure 4-A? Or was it difficult trying to think about who you are outside of being the owner of your company?

This Identity Exercise can help you become more aware of how emotionally connected you are to your identity as owner of your company.

Figure 4-A

The Identity Exercise

Outside of My Work....

1. What do I enjoy doing?
2. What gives my life meaning?
3. What do I honor and respect myself for?
4. What do I admire myself for?
5. What do I appreciate about myself?
6. What do I like about myself?
7. What do I deserve praise for?
8. I am valuable for the following reasons:
9. What good things have other people said about me over the years?
10. In addition to my work, what am I good at?
11. What am I really proud of about myself?
12. Why am I a good person?

Expanding Your Thinking about Who You Are and Who You Can Become

After doing the Life-Transitions and Identity Exercises, reflect on how you feel.

- Have these two exercises helped you feel more positive or hopeful when you think about your future transitions?
- Does your mind now feel more open and flexible?
- Do you feel that new opportunities may be awaiting you?

The next two chapters will help you expand your thinking about your future possibilities even further.

CHAPTER 5

It's not "Retirement," it's "The Platinum Years[SM]" – a New Stage of Active Life for Baby Boomers

What Comes Before the "Golden Years?"

For previous generations, leaving one's work meant retiring and moving into the "Golden Years." But as we all know, those so-called "Golden Years" after retiring are usually assumed to be years of decline, when we age, lose our abilities and are no longer able to contribute productively to the world. The typical image of the "Golden Years" is of an old person sent "out to pasture" – someone who plays golf all day or sits on the porch in a rocking chair.

But because of the unique history of the Baby Boomer generation, in combination with new discoveries about the causes of aging and decline, the fact is that for Baby Boomers this is not the future we have to live. Because millions of Baby Boomers are beginning to enter their 50s and 60s, much new research is now being done about what causes aging and how we can strengthen and expand the active, productive stage of our lives.

Several recent studies have discovered that Baby Boomers who leave their work are not leaving in order to "retire" and decline. Instead, Baby Boomers in their 50s and 60s are entering a new stage of active, meaningful life. As a May 2, 2007 article in Knowledge@Wharton explained, "Unlike their parents and grandparents, many baby boomers will never retire in the traditional sense," said [Michael] Milken, who argues that this is all to the good. "They are young, and they are going to stay young. Medical advances are just one factor," he noted. In addition, attitudes have changed. Decades ago, the media portrayed women in the 40s and 50s as elderly; now it shows them as young and active. 'So, yes, it's good news. Eighty is the new 60…Sixty is the new 40."

STPI calls this active new stage of life "The Platinum Years[SM]." And this stage of active, meaningful life can continue for another 10, 20 or 30 years. (See Figure 5-A.)

Figure 5-A

How Baby Boomers Are Redefining Retirement

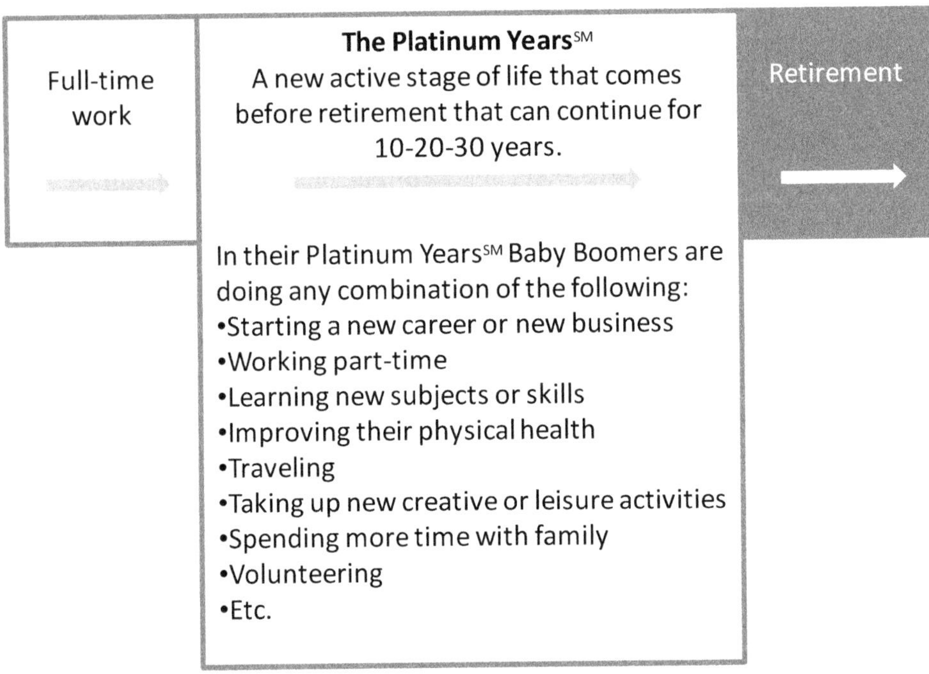

New Discoveries about Aging and Health

The ability of Baby Boomers to live meaningful and healthy new lives into our 50s, 60s, 70s or beyond is supported by exciting new research into the causes of aging and new information about the sources of continued mental and physical health and well-being.

One of the most important new discoveries is that what we think of as "aging" often results from our feeling that we are useless and have nothing to offer.

In addition to taking care of yourself physically – for example through regular physical exercise and enjoying healthy food – scientists are now discovering that some of the most important factors that can contribute to our continued health and full mental functioning are psychological and social factors, even as we age. For example, scientists are now discovering that people who feel they are making a difference in the world, or who have rewarding relationships and are part of supportive social networks, are both physically and mentally healthier than people who feel useless or are isolated and alone. These psychological and social factors apply to people of any age, and are especially relevant to Baby Boomers as we grow older.

Scientists are now discovering that some of the most important factors that can contribute to our continued health and full mental functioning are psychological and social factors, even as we age.

And this means that the decisions you make about what you will do in your future life can affect not only your future happiness, but also your future health and well-being.

Some of these provocative new discoveries are described below. (References about how Baby Boomers are redefining "retirement" and the new discoveries about aging and health are in the "Resources" section at the end of this book.)

Our Brains Continue to Grow

One of the most important of these recent scientific discoveries is the new understanding that no matter how old you are, your brain continues to grow. The innate ability of your brain to continually grow new nerve cells and create new connections between them – which allows you to keep learning and expanding your mental abilities – is called "neuroplasticity."

A basic principle of brain-plasticity is that in order for your brain to keep growing, you have to regularly engage in mentally stimulating activities. Furthermore, these activities have to keep providing your brain with new and different experiences. Merely doing crossword puzzles every day is not going to stimulate your brain to its maximum development, and spending every day simply playing golf will not do it, either.

This means that your plan for your new life needs to provide you with a range of interesting and meaningful new experiences. Not only will this make you happier. It will also help your brain keep continually active and growing.

Our Muscles Can Remain Strong

Another common stereotype of older people is that we will lose our physical strength. But the new research into aging also contradicts this assumption.

New research is showing that regular physical exercise can keep our bodies in good shape at any age. And even if you are an older person who has gotten out of shape, beginning a new regimen of moderate but regular physical exercise, which includes strength-training and regular weight-bearing activities such as walking or dancing, can help restore or even increase your muscular development and physical strength.

Your Mental and Emotional Well-Being Affect Your Physical Health

Another important new set of discoveries is about the interconnections among our mental and emotional well-being and our physical health. The most familiar example of this is the impact of emotionally-caused stress on physical health.

As much new research is now revealing, being under emotional stress activates your body's fight-or-flight mechanism. Continued activation of fight-or-flight causes ongoing release of your body's stress hormones, such as adrenaline and cortisol, into the bloodstream, which eventually causes wear and tear on your body. Continual stress is associated with many different – and potentially dangerous – physical ailments, such as ulcers, high-blood pressure, heart disease and diabetes.

Although work can be stressful, having a lonely and unfulfilling life after leaving your work can also be emotionally stressful and can also cause harmful physical results and poor health. This is another reason why creating an emotionally fulfilling and meaningful new life for yourself after leaving your company is so important.

Your Relationships and Social Connections Affect Both Your Emotional and Physical Well-Being

One of the most fascinating new discoveries is about how our social relationships and involvement with other people can affect our physical health and well-being.

Much new research is revealing that people who have supportive relationships or who feel part of a supportive community tend to be physically healthier as a result than people who are socially isolated or lonely. It is now well-documented that having supportive social connections helps reduce the harmful effects of stress on the mind and body, and that people with supportive social relationships actually tend to get sick less often and heal more quickly. Research even suggests that people who engage in regular social relationships are less likely to develop Alzheimer's than people who are lonely.

New research is also demonstrating that people who spend time helping others can gain both improved emotional and physical health as a result. This effect is called the "Helper's High."

A New Paradigm for Your Platinum Years℠

You can benefit from all of these new discoveries by incorporating their lessons into your plans for your Platinum Years℠.

What new opportunities will open up for you, when you decide to transition out of your role as owner of your company and plan for how you can improve your physical, mental and emotional well-being in your Platinum Years℠?

CHAPTER 6

Why Your Personal Transition Plan Is the Essential First Step for a Successful Business Transition

Successful transition planning requires two separate plans – your Personal Transition Plan and your Business Transition Plan. The process begins by creating your Personal Transition Plan.

Your Personal Transition Plan comes first for three reasons:

1. Personal Financial Planning:
   A clear vision and comprehensive, detailed plan for your new life lets you and your financial advisors accurately determine how much money you will need for your future. This allows you and your personal financial planner or wealth management advisor to do more accurate financial planning for your future life.

2. Business Transition Planning:
   Knowing how much money you will need for your new life gives you a firm financial goal to aim for in your business transition strategy.

3. Emotional confidence:
   Having a clear and comprehensive vision of your new life gives you a positive new future to look forward to, and helps you transition more confidently and successfully out of your life as an owner. (See Figure 6-A.)

Figure 6-A

Your Personal Transition Plan Comes First

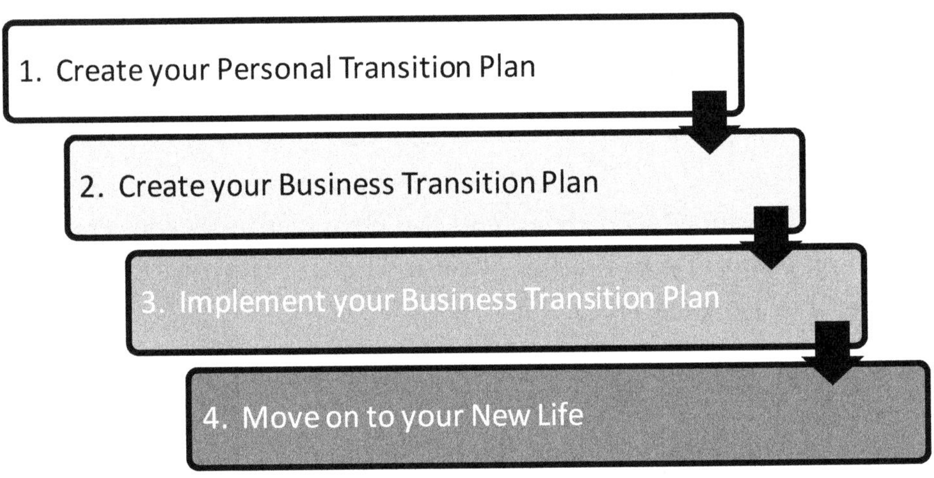

Creating Your Personal Transition Goals

Your Personal Transition Plan begins with creating your Personal Transition Goals. Seven key questions will help you create these goals:

1. When do you want to leave your company?

2. What do you want to do with your life after you leave your company?

3. How much money will you need to support your new life?

4. How much money can come from your personal assets and investments?

5. How much money will you need from your company?

6. Have you done your estate planning?
   If yes - How does your estate plan support and sustain your vision?
   If not – When will I do it, and with whom?

7. Have you done the planning needed to minimize your personal taxes?
   If not – When will I do it, and with whom?

Figure 6-B will help you focus your thinking on these Personal Transition Goals. The rest of this chapter describes the information you need to obtain and the actions you need to take in order to answer each of these questions in 6-B.

Figure 6-B

My Personal Transition Planning Goals

1. When do I want to leave my company?	
2. What do I want to do with my life after I leave?	
3. How much money will I need to support my new life? • How much can come from my personal assets and investments?	
4. How much money will I need from my company?	
5. Have I done my needed estate planning? If yes: • How does my estate plan support and sustain my vision? If not: • When will I do it? • And with whom?	
6. Have I done the needed planning to minimize my personal taxes? If not: • When am I doing it? • And with whom?	

When do you plan to leave your company?

A key personal transition goal is deciding when you will leave your company. Here are several methods that owners use to decide on a departure date:

- Choose a specific year when you want to leave
- The age when you want to leave
- When your company has achieved a specific level of sales
- The time it will take to implement your business transition strategy (2 to 5 years)
- The time it will take to increase the value of your business, so that when you leave it can provide you with the money you will need

Of course you should also discuss with your spouse (or with other family members) when they want you to move out of your life as an owner and transition into your new life.

Which method will you use to choose your planned departure date?

Also keep in mind that you can always change your planned departure date later on if circumstances change. But it's important to choose a specific departure date now, as part of your Personal Transition Goals, because this gives you a firm goal to aim toward and will make the rest of your planning and implementation process more solid and real.

Estate Planning and Personal Tax Planning

If you have not yet done your estate planning, now is the time to do so. Work with your personal financial planner or wealth management advisor and with an estate attorney to do estate planning and minimize your personal taxes as you move through the Transition Process.

Estate planning is a deeply personal process, and you want to find an estate planning attorney with whom you feel comfortable. If you don't already have an estate attorney, get references from your friends, other family members and from your CPA and investment advisor – then go out and interview several attorneys to get a sense of what they offer and with whom you will want to work.

Your objectives in estate planning will include: protecting your family, creating a financial legacy, minimizing taxes, and other personal objectives such as philanthropic donations, etc. Your estate attorney will work with you to determine what assets you want to protect (your home, investments and savings, retirement plans, etc.), who you want to receive your assets after you are gone, and the best strategies and vehicles for protecting your assets.

Personal tax planning should be done as part of estate planning. If you are planning to transfer your company to new owners, inform your estate attorney of your intention, since this will impact your estate and personal tax planning.

You may also want to explore the Purposeful Planning Institute of Denver, CO, www.purposefulplanninginstitute.com , a network of estate and wealth management professionals who emphasize helping their clients realize their deepest personal intentions – including your personal and ethical values – through the process of planning for and transferring your wealth to your heirs.

Determining Your Future Financial Needs

The money you will need for your future life after leaving your company is your "Personal Financial Goal." Having a clear and comprehensive vision and plan for your new life is essential for determining how much money you will need for this new life. (The last part of this chapter explains how you can create this personal vision and plan.)

After you have designed your plan for your new future, meet with your personal financial planner/wealth management advisor and show them your plan. This will allow your professional financial advisors to determine how much money you will need for your future life.

Your Personal Financial Goal can include other financial intentions you may have for your future in addition to supporting your future lifestyle – for example, you may also want to help pay your grandchildren's college tuition, make a philanthropic donation to a favorite community or charitable organization, etc.

How much money can come from your personal assets and investments?

Once your financial advisors have determined how much money you will need, they can determine if your current personal assets and investments will provide enough to support your new life.

If you already have sufficient personal assets to support your future plans, you are fortunate indeed. Not only can you more successfully live the new personal future you have envisioned. Being able to support your new life from your personal assets can also give you more flexibility in designing and implementing your Business Transition Plan (see Part III).

If your current personal assets and investments will not fully be able to support your planned new future, this means that you have a "Personal Financial Gap." Your financial advisors may be able to redesign your investment strategies in order to bring you the future income you will need.

But that may still not be enough.

How much money will you need from your company?

If you have a Personal Financial Gap, part of your future income may need to come from the money you will get from transferring your company to new owners. Figure 6-C graphically summarizes how your future financial needs relate to your Business Transition Process.

As part of your Business Transition Process you will need to have a business valuation done for your company, to determine how much money your company is worth to potential new owners. You may also discover that you will need to improve the operations of your company in order to make it more attractive to new owners or to ensure that the company can provide you with the future income you will need after you have left your position as owner. Part III explains more about how to successfully plan for and implement these and other essential business transition issues.

Figure 6-C

How Your Future Personal Financial Needs Relate to Your Business Transition Process

<table>
<tr><td>1. Determine your Personal Financial Goal for your new future. (How much money you will need for your new life, plus any additional future financial goals you may have.)</td></tr>
<tr><td>2. Evaluate your Personal Assets and Investments.
<ul>
<li>Will your Personal Assets and Investments be enough to cover your future Personal Financial Goal?</li>
<li>Do you have a Personal Financial <u>Gap</u>? If yes, how will you fill this gap?</li>
<li>Can you increase your Personal Assets and Investments to meet your Personal Financial Goal?</li>
</ul>
If that will still not be enough,
<ul>
<li>How much money will you need from your business (from transitioning the company to new owners) to cover your Personal Financial Gap?</li>
</ul></td></tr>
<tr><td>3. The amount of money you will need from the Business Transition Process is your "Financial Transition Goal."</td></tr>
</table>

Designing a Comprehensive Vision of Your Personal Future

The centerpiece of your Personal Transition Plan is a comprehensive, detailed vision and plan for a new life that you can't wait to live – a new future that will bring you a sense of meaning and purpose even when you are no longer running your company.

In order to create an effective and meaningful plan for your future life it is essential for you to expand your thinking about your future possibilities. Since most owners have not spent much time thinking about life after being an owner, they don't have many ideas about what could be included in their new life. Also, if you have focused most of your time, energy and intelligence on the challenge of running your company successfully, you probably have a limited perspective on what else you could do with your life.

To create an exciting and meaningful new life that you can't wait to live, you need to see yourself as a "whole person," with physical, intellectual, financial, emotional, family, social, and even spiritual needs.

STPI's Integrative Transition Planning methods help you expand your thinking about your future by having you think about 10 different areas of your future life, then brainstorming many different options that you could do in each of these 10 lifestyle-areas. Only after you have expanded your thinking significantly in all of these ways should you make your decisions about what you will do in each of these 10 lifestyle-areas and plan for how you will implement each of your decisions.

The rest of this chapter will help you expand your thinking about the new opportunities available to you in each of these 10 lifestyle-areas. Some of these 10 lifestyle-areas may seem obvious, while for others you may wonder "Why do I need to think about this?" Before you close out any options, first explore each area through the questions below. You may still decide that some of the 10 lifestyle-areas presented here are not appropriate for you, but take a chance and explore them all first.

To do this brainstorming exercise, take 10 pieces of paper. At the top of each page write the name of one of the lifestyle-areas listed below. Then in the order in which these 10 lifestyle-areas are presented, think about and answer the questions for that area.

1. Physical Health Activity

Reasons for doing a Physical Health Activity: Essential for good physical health and physical well-being; good physical health supports good mental and emotional health; essential for your overall well-being.

- Types of Physical Health Activities: Physical exercise, good nutrition, adequate rest and relaxation, stress-reduction.

- Are you currently doing any kind of Physical Health Activity?
  What do you like about doing it?
  What do you not like about doing it?

- Brainstorm some specific Physical Health Activities you would like to do in your new life. (For example: walking, bicycling, joining a health club, doing yoga, canoeing, etc.)

- Write down your ideas for Physical Health Activities you could do in your new life.

2. Intellectual Stimulation

Reasons for doing an Intellectually Stimulating Activity: Your work has been a major source of intellectual stimulation in your life. Because ongoing mental stimulation will help to keep your brain active and growing (see Chapter 5), then for your optimum well-being and to continue a life of meaning and purpose, you need to develop a new source of intellectual stimulation in your new life.

- Types of Intellectually Stimulating Activities: Learning new skills, acquiring new information, teaching others, engaging with others in intellectually challenging activities, seeking out intellectually-expanding new experiences.

- Are you currently doing any kind of Intellectually Stimulating Activity outside of your work?
  What do you like about doing it?
  What do you not like about doing it?

- Brainstorm some specific Intellectually Stimulating Activities you would like to do in your new life. (For example: Attend college classes on subjects of interest, share my specialized knowledge, join a book club or chess club, go on archaeological digs, etc.)

- Write down your ideas for Intellectually Stimulating Activities you could do in your new life.

3. Recreational/Creative Activity

Reasons for doing a Recreational/Creative Activity: Recreational and creative activities can provide physical rejuvenation, mental stimulation, a sense of competitive achievement, an opportunity for creative self-expression, the ability to enjoy social interactions, and/or being able to have fun like a kid.

- Types of Recreational/Creative Activities: Enjoyable physical activity, intellectually stimulating activity done for fun, spectator appreciation, having a social life – fun with friends, solitary experience – for relaxation, self-deepening or self-expansion.

- Are you currently doing any kind of Recreational or Creative Activity?

  What do you like about doing it?
  What do you not like about doing it?

- Brainstorm some specific Recreational/Creative Activities you would like to do in your new life. (Examples: Play a musical instrument, join a band, coach Little League, go hiking or bird-watching, do classic car restoration, etc.)

- Write down your ideas for Recreational/Creative Activities you could do in your new life.

4. Activity with Your Spouse/Partner

In your new life you will be able to spend more time doing enjoyable, meaningful activities with your spouse. As part of creating your Personal Transition Plan, discuss with your spouse what activities the two of you would enjoy doing together.

- Brainstorm some specific activities you and your spouse would like to do together in your new life. (Examples: Travel to other countries, buy season tickets to local plays, go ballroom dancing, take art classes together, etc.)

- Write down your ideas for activities you and your spouse would like to do together.

5. Activity with Other Family Members

You may also have other family members, such as your children, your parents, your grandchildren, siblings or other relatives with whom you want to spend more time.

- Write down the name of each relative with whom you want to spend more time in your new life.
- For each relative you named, brainstorm an activity that you want to do with them and write it down.

6. Residence – Where You Want to Live

You may want to continue living where you live now. Or you may want to move to a new home or new location. Here are some questions to help you consider where you want to make your future residence. Do any of these apply to you? Write down all the reasons that apply.

- Want a better climate/better physical environment
- Want to be near family members
- Want a lower cost of living

- Want to downsize/current home is too big
- Want to upscale to a dream house
- Want to live in a retirement community
- Want to move because of health reasons
- Ideas for where to live: Move to a different part of the U.S., stay in your current home and also get a second home in a different area, move to a small town or college town, move to a different country.
- Brainstorm some specific ideas for where you would like to live in your new life. Write down your ideas.

7. Social Connections

Reasons for creating Social Connections in your new life: Scientific research has shown that people who enjoy regular social connections have better physical, mental and emotional health than lonely individuals (see Chapter 5).

Your work gives you social connections and relationships – with employees, customers, vendors, colleagues in your field, etc. But after owners leave their companies, they usually lose contact with their former work colleagues, because they no longer have work issues in common.

If you found your social connections and relationships from work gratifying, then for your optimum well-being and feelings of meaning and purpose, you will want to create a new source of social connections in your new life.

You cannot expect your family members to fill in this social gap. In your new life you will need to either maintain your former social connections, or build new social connections in addition to your family.

- Examples of activities to build Social Connections: Neighborhood/community events, sports leagues, "Meet-up" groups, your college or high school alumni association.

- Outside of your work, do you currently have other social connections or are you doing some kind of social activity?
  What do you like about doing it?
  What do you not like about doing it?

- Brainstorm some specific activities you could do in your new life to help you stay connected to other people. (Examples: Card-playing group, local historical society, coach a youth league, garden club, "Friends of the Library," etc.)

- Write down your ideas for activities you could do to stay socially connected in your new life.

8. Spirituality/Faith

Reasons for thinking about Spirituality/Faith: For many individuals, their spirituality or faith is an important source of meaning and purpose in their lives. Whether or not you belong to an organized religion, you may have spiritual feelings about the world, the universe, your role in the world or the deeper purpose of your life.

As you create a meaningful plan for your new future, you have the opportunity to explore, expand and deepen your spirituality.

- Do you consider yourself a <u>Religious</u> person?

- Do you consider yourself a <u>Spiritual</u> person?

- Are you currently doing any kind of activity to express your Spirituality or Faith?
  What do you like about doing it?
  What do you <u>not</u> like about doing it?

- Examples of ways to explore or express your Spirituality/Faith: Books or classes on spiritual topics, spiritual study groups, meditation, thinking deeply about life, spending time in Nature, helping others.

- Brainstorm some specific activities you would like to do to express your Spirituality/Faith in your new life. (Examples: Learn to meditate, join a committee at my religious institution, take long walks in Nature, give back to my community, etc.)

- Write down your ideas for how you could express your Spirituality/Faith in your new life.

9. Income-Producing Work

Some owners may absolutely <u>not</u> want to include any further income-producing work in their new lives. Others may want to include some type of income-producing work – perhaps part-time work – in their plan for a new life. The choice of whether or not to do future income-producing work depends on your specific circumstances.

Here are some reasons why you might want to do some type of income-producing work in your future. Do any of these apply to you? Write down all the reasons that apply.

- To keep active and engaged
- Need the income to live on
- To maintain my current lifestyle
- Want income to enjoy extras
- To keep being mentally active
- To keep physically active
- To maintain connections with others
- Health insurance benefits
- If you do want to work, explore new work possibilities. Check out www.notyetretired.com for stories about working "retirees."
- Brainstorm some specific types of Income-Producing Work you would like to do in your new life.
- Write down these ideas for Income-Producing Work you could do in your new life.

10. Volunteer/Philanthropic Activity

Reasons for thinking about doing a Volunteer/Philanthropic Activity: Scientific research has documented that activities such as helping others and giving back to your community can actually improve your mental, emotional and physical health. (See Chapter 5.)

There may be some specific philanthropic cause or community issue that you would like to be more involved with. Or maybe volunteer work is new to you. As you create your plan for a meaningful and fulfilling new life, consider if you want to include a Volunteer or Philanthropic Activity as part of this plan.

- Examples of Volunteer/Philanthropic Activities: Youth or education programs, community service organizations, teaching others, arts, protecting the environment, hospitals or health-related organizations, international volunteering.

- Are you currently doing any kind of Volunteer/Philanthropic Activity?

  What do you like about doing it?
  What do you not like about doing it?

- Brainstorm some specific Volunteer/Philanthropic Activities you would like to do in your new life. (Examples: Participate in a tutoring program, work at a museum, help in a local homeless shelter or soup kitchen, Habitat for Humanity, Peace Corps, etc.)

- Write down your ideas for Volunteer or Philanthropic Activities you could do in your new life.

Making Decisions for Your New Life

After brainstorming each of the 10 lifestyle-areas above, place all 10 sheets of paper on which you've written these ideas in front of you and look them over. Do you see any common patterns among them? Move the 10 pieces of paper around. Which of your ideas are especially compatible with or supportive of other ideas? Note which ideas feel like they would work best for you, and which would make your new life the most fulfilling and enjoyable.

Now look over your 10 brainstorming sheets again. Choose and circle your top idea in each of these 10 lifestyle-areas.

Take another sheet of paper, and copy onto it the 10 statements in Figure 6-D. Now fill in this new sheet with the top 10 activities you've chosen – one activity for each lifestyle-area.

(Note: If you want to do more than one activity for a specific lifestyle-area, write down the additional activities that will also be part of your plan. And if you have decided that any of these 10 lifestyle-areas is not relevant to your new life, just leave that line blank.)

Figure 6-D

My 10 Decisions for My Future Life.

1. The Physical Health Activity I will do:
2. The activity I will do for Intellectual Stimulation:
3. The Recreational/Creative Activity I will do:
4. The activity I will do with my Spouse/Partner:
5. The activity I will do with other Family Members:
6. This is where I want to live:
7. The activity I will do to stay Socially Connected:
8. The activity I will do to express my Spirituality/Faith:
9. The Income-Producing Work I will do:
10. The Volunteer/Philanthropic Activity I will do:

Vision of a New Life You Can't Wait to Live

Now take some time to look over the 10 lifestyle-decisions you have just made.

Can you imagine yourself living a new life characterized by all of these new activities? How does that make you feel? Are you excited by this new possibility?

Are you ready to explore how you can make this vision a reality?

Part III describes the next steps for you to take, so you can move into this new life.

FINDING YOUR NEW OWNER

PART III

HOW TO CREATE A SUCCESSFUL BUSINESS TRANSITION
THAT WILL BRING YOU A NEW LIFE OF MEANING AND PURPOSE

CHAPTER 7

Thinking Like a CEO

Your company is your "baby." Perhaps you founded it or you brought it to its current level of success, and as a result, you have deep emotional ties to it.

Being owner of your company also brings you many rewards – financial, emotional and social. Your role as owner provides you with feelings of accomplishment, self-esteem, being in charge, being a leader, gives your life a sense of meaning and purpose, provides you with the opportunity to be creative, gives you social status and brings you relationships with your employees, customers, vendors, etc.

For all these reasons you have strong emotional connections to your company and it can be difficult to let it go, difficult to think about passing it on to new ownership.

Here's an analogy: A business owner who is preparing for the Business Transition Process is like a parent. You've spent many years raising your child and helping her grow, and now your child is getting ready to leave home – she is going to get married, she is going to move into a new life and someone else will now become the central person in your child's life. It's understandable why this transition would be emotionally difficult for you.

Here's another analogy: A business owner preparing for the Business Transition Process is like a boat-builder. You've spent many years designing the boat and many years actually building it. You're proud of what you've created, but now you have to launch that boat. You have to bring it to the water's edge and let it go, with a new captain at the helm. It can be emotionally painful to let go.

Your business is your "baby." You've spent many years raising this child, helping her grow, and now your child is getting ready to leave home – she is going to get married, she is going to move into a new life. Someone else will now become the central person in your child's life. It's understandable why this transition would be emotionally difficult for you.

As Chapter 3 explained, the Business Transition Process is a transition for both you and your company. It is a transition from a company owned and run by you, to a company with new ownership. It is not only a technical, financial and transactional process; it is also a personal and an emotional process.

The Business Transition Process may involve new goals for your company, improvements in your company's operations and new organizational structure – changes that will allow the company to continue successfully when you are no longer running it. You need to feel comfortable with these types of changes. You also need to be emotionally ready to think strategically about how you will transition out of your business so the transition will be successful – both for you and for the future of the company.

Honoring Your Accomplishments

Reflecting on what you've accomplished and appreciating what you've created in your company can help you feel more comfortable with letting go of your "baby." Here are several questions to help you recognize and honor your achievements.

Your accomplishments: As the owner of your company, what have you accomplished that you are proud of? What have you created that you feel good about? (for example – good products, high customer satisfaction, a good living for your family, a good reputation in your industry, generating many employment opportunities, a good corporate culture, good relationships with your work colleagues, community involvement, etc.)

Your legacy: What in your company would you like to see continued after you have moved on?

Take some time to think about these questions and write down your answers.

Now read over and reflect on your answers. How do they make you feel? – proud? other emotions?

You have much to feel good about, and much to be proud of.

Thinking Like a CEO

Chapter 4 showed you how to use Transition Thinking to expand your thinking about your personal identity. Now we will use Transition

Thinking to help you expand your thinking about the future of your company.

Transition Thinking for your company is different from the type of thinking you use in the day-to-day running of your business. Transition Thinking for your business means taking a long-term view of the future of your company – thinking like a CEO, not only like a COO.

The CEO – Chief Executive Officer – is the highest ranking individual at a firm. As the person ultimately responsible for the success or failure of the business, the CEO's job is to think long-term, see the Big Picture and provide overall strategic direction for the firm. The CEO is a visionary leader who looks at the future to discover or develop new opportunities for change that will increase the company's success.

The COO – Chief Operating Officer – is the executive responsible for the day-to-day operations of the firm. The COO's job is to keep the nitty-gritty, nuts-and-bolts issues of the company operating successfully. The COO is responsible for ensuring that business operations are efficient and effective, overseeing the proper management of resources and the distribution of goods and services to customers, and keeping employees skilled and motivated.

The CEO creates the larger vision, and the COO keeps the company in line with the CEO's vision.

As the owner of your company, you are its CEO. However, you are probably focused primarily on day-to-day operations. In the day-to-day running of the business, most owners usually think and act like the COO – dealing with short-term issues, constantly tackling immediate problems and trying to meet immediate goals.

However, as your company's CEO you are also responsible for stepping back from the day-to-day activities so you can take broader, long-range issues into consideration, think about and plan for the future direction of your company and create a long-term vision for its future success.

A company's Chief Executive Officer creates the larger vision for where the company is going, and its Chief Operating Officer keeps the company in line with the CEO's vision. You probably think and act primarily like the Chief Operating Officer, focused on the day-to-day operations of the company. But as the owner you are also its CEO, responsible for stepping back from the day-to-day activities so you can think about and plan for the future direction of your company and create a long-term vision for its success. It's not easy to think about the long-term success of your company at the same time as you are planning to transition out of it – that's your challenge.

It's difficult enough to do all that when you are constantly immersed in the daily operations. It's especially challenging to think about your company's long-term success at the same time as you personally are planning to transition out of the company. But that's your new challenge as CEO.

Can your company run successfully without you?

Here's a mental experiment to help you think like a CEO.

> As your company's owner, you are involved in many aspects of its operations. If you suddenly left the company without any preparation or warning, could the company continue to run successfully without you?

As an owner preparing for the Business Transition Process, you need to recognize the many different kinds of work you do now for the company, the many roles you play and the many ways in which you assure the company's success.

Take some time to reflect on the following question and write down your answers:

> What activities do I perform now for the successful operation of my company? (List as many answers as you can. For example – day-to-day decisions, customer relations, managing employees, hiring employees, product development, sales, marketing, financial decisions, long-term planning for the future of the company, etc.)

Now think about this question:

> Can I imagine someone else filling all these roles and successfully running the company?

You can answer this question intellectually, by recognizing all that you do for the company and thinking about how to find someone to replace you.

You can also answer this question from an emotional perspective:

> When you think about someone else running your company so it continues to be successful after you have moved on, what emotions do you feel? Do you feel pleased? Sad? A little of both?

Thinking about the Best New Owner

Here's another mental experiment to help you both think like a CEO and feel more emotionally prepared for the Business Transition Process.

- Imagine that you have found the best new owner for your company. The process of transferring your company to this new owner has provided you with all the money you will need for your future and you are now enjoying your new life, while this best new owner is now running the company successfully.
- What characteristics does this new owner have?
- What activities is this new owner doing?
- How do your employees feel about this new owner?
- How do the customers feel about this new owner?

Note: In this mental experiment, your "best new owner" is not someone you already know. Think of it as someone you have not met yet, who has all the characteristics you want the new owner to have.

You may not get everything you want in the new owner. But the more clear and complete your vision of what you want in the new owner of your company, the more likely you are to get it.

Now take some time to think about the questions above and write down the ideas that come to you.

What emotions did you feel while you were doing this exercise?

It may not be possible for you to achieve all your results. But just imagining them is an important step toward planning for and achieving a successful Business Transition Process.

The scenario you've just imagined may also stimulate new ideas in you and help expand your thinking about future possibilities. And it will certainly help you become more aware of your emotions about the Transition Process, so they don't unexpectedly sabotage you.

Thinking Like the CEO of Your New Life: Process Goals and Outcome Goals

Achieving a successful business transition requires that you create two sets of goals – process goals and outcome goals.

Your process goals are the goals you will need to accomplish during each step of the Business Transition Process in order to transition successfully. Process goals include transactional issues such as these:

> Work with my financial advisors to determine my Financial Transition Goal – the amount of money I will need from the company to support my new life.
>
> Do a business valuation to determine the current value of my company.
>
> If the current value of the company is not enough to meet my Financial Transition Goal, develop a plan for increasing my company's value so that by the time I am ready to leave, the value of my company will be high enough to support my Financial Transition Goal.
>
> Determine who would be the best new owner for the company – an owner who will be able to provide me with the income I need for my Financial Transition Goal, and who will keep the company running successfully after I've left.
>
> Make the company have value for and be attractive to a new owner.
>
> If the new owner I have chosen will not be able to pay me the company's value up-front when I leave, I will have to negotiate a

deferred payment plan that meets my needs – which includes how much money I will need and when I will receive it.

Outcome goals are the end results that you want to achieve through your Business Transition Process. These can include goals for yourself and your family, and also goals for the company. Outcome goals can be either financial or non-financial (for example: related to your quality of life, emotional satisfaction or ethical values). Examples of your outcome goals might include:

- Leave by my desired departure date.
- Leave with enough money to support my Financial Transition Goal.
- Be able to create a fulfilling new life for myself and my family after I've left the company.
- Find a new owner who will appreciate and continue the special characteristics and values I've created in the company (continuing my legacy).

Achieving Your Transition Goals

The rest of this book explains how to design and achieve both your process and outcome goals through the Business Transition Process.

Chapter 8 begins with a strategic overview of the entire Transition Process, including personal aspects, business aspects, financial aspects, process goals, outcome goals and how the various aspects relate to each other.

CHAPTER 8

Expanding Your Thinking about the Transition Process

As the owner of your company, you are ultimately in charge of the Transition Process. You will need to bring in experienced advisors to help you plan and implement various parts of the process, but ultimately it is all about meeting your needs.

In order to guide the Transition Process successfully, you will need to:

1. Think both intellectually and emotionally about your needs.
2. Gather information.
3. Analyze information.
4. Make decisions and create your transition goals.
5. Develop strategic plans for implementing your decisions and achieving your goals.

6. Periodically re-assess where you are in the Transition Process, and if any changes need to be made to your goals, plans or implementation.
7. Bring in professional advisors to help with specific steps of the Transition Process, including help with information gathering, analysis, planning and implementing your plans.
8. Repeat each of the above activities as needed, until you have successfully completed your Transition Process.

Your Business Transition Strategic Plan

Just as you need to create a detailed, comprehensive written Personal Transition Plan for your personal future in order to assure that you achieve it successfully, you also need a detailed, comprehensive written plan for your Business Transition Process.

A successful Business Transition Strategic Plan should cover a range of business, personal and financial issues. For example, it should include:

Your future personal financial needs.

How much money do you need or want from your company by transferring it to new ownership (your Financial Transition Goal)?

Other personal, financial and business goals that you want to achieve through the Business Transition Process.

Is the current value of your company enough to meet your Financial Transition Goal?

An evaluation of your company's readiness for transition, and a strategy for improving your company's readiness.

If your company is not ready now for transfer to new owners, how can you increase its value or improve its operations so transferring it to new ownership will provide you with the money you want?

Who would be the best new owner for your company?

A strategy for transferring your company successfully to that new owner.

You Are Not Alone: The Transition Advisors Who Can Help You Create a Successful Transition Process

The typical Transition Process can take 2 to 5 years. Many different issues need to be decided, plans made, and actions taken in order to successfully design and implement a successful Transition Process. It takes time to:

- Think about and develop your Personal and Business Transition Goals.
- Assemble your advisory team.
- Create your Personal and Business Transition Plans.
- Prepare your company for transition.
- Find or train the best new owner.
- Negotiate the deal.

That's why having a team of experienced transition advisors is so important. Different advisors can help you plan and implement the various steps of the process. Advisors:

- Have experience and expertise in specific aspects of the Transition Process that you do not have.
- Can provide you with the business and financial information you need to make crucial decisions and can help you design and implement your transition goals.
- Can help you improve the operations of your company so it will be more attractive and valuable to new owners.
- Can help you find and negotiate with new owners so you get the best financial and other desired outcomes.

Your advisors can focus their energies and apply their expertise to their special areas of the Transition Process, so you can keep your attention focused on running the company day-to-day, and preparing it for transition while making sure that your goals remain paramount in the overall process.

An Integrated Overview of the Transition Process

Because the Transition Process is so complex, with so many different issues to be considered, it can seem overwhelming. In order to help you get a handle on what is involved, STPI breaks the overall Transition Process into four parallel "Transition Tracks," all running simultaneously.

Your Personal Transition Process: The activities involved in designing and implementing your personal plan for a meaningful and fulfilling new future.

Personal Financial Planning: The activities involved in determining your personal financial needs, improving your personal assets and investments and doing estate planning and personal tax planning.

The Business Transition Process: The activities involved in establishing your business transition goals, analyzing your options for new ownership, improving the value of your company, finding or preparing the new owner, negotiating the deal, etc., so the outcome of the Business Transition Process provides you with the money you will need for your future life and allows you to feel you have made the best decision for the company.

The Business Continuation Process: The activities involved in keeping your business running successfully day-to-day while you are looking for a new owner and preparing the company for transition.

Figures 8-A through 8-E present a simplified overview depicting five key stages of the Transition Process:

Stage One:	Becoming mentally and emotionally prepared
Stage Two:	Getting ready to plan
Stage Three	Creating your Business Transition Plan
Stage Four:	Implementing your Business Transition Plan
Stage Five:	Negotiating the deal

In each stage you will see the four Transition Tracks, key activities and decisions in each track, and the professional advisors who can help with these activities. (A more detailed overview could have included many other transition activities in addition to those presented here.)

Figures 8-A through 8-E are only a general guide to how the overall Transition Process might unfold. The steps may be different for you if you entered the process at one of the later stages, and you may now have to go back to complete some of the earlier activities. Or you may be working with an advisor or advisory team who has brought you into the

Transition Process and who may have already done some of the earlier stages with you.

Figure 8-A

Becoming Mentally and Emotionally Prepared

Stage One of the Transition Process

The Four Transition Tracks	Activities	Transition Advisors Who Can Help You
Personal Transition Process:	Become mentally and emotionally prepared to think about your future personal and business transitions.	Your Transition Planning Consultant
	Design your Personal Transition Plan for a new life you can't wait to live, and create your Personal Transition Goals.	Your Transition Planning Consultant
Personal Financial Planning:	Determine how much money you will need for your new life. • Will your personal assets and investments be enough to support your new life? • Do you have a "Personal Financial Gap?"	Your Personal Financial Planner or Wealth Management Advisor
	How much money will you need from your company to support your new life (your "Financial Transition Goal")?	Your Personal Financial Planner or Wealth Management Advisor
Business Transition Process:	Get all your business records in order.	Your business attorney and CPA
Business Continuation Process:	Get all your business records in order.	Your business attorney and CPA

Figure 8-B

Getting Ready to Plan

Stage Two of the Transition Process

The Four Transition Tracks	Activities	Transition Advisors Who Can Help You
Personal Transition Process:	Think about and design your Personal, Business and Financial Goals that you want to achieve through the Business Transition Process.	Your Transition Planning Consultant
Personal Financial Planning:	Do your estate planning and personal tax planning.	Your Personal Financial Planner and Estate Attorney
Business Transition Process:	Analyze your options for new ownership and decide on the best option for your new owner.	Your Transition Planning Consultant
	Do a Business Valuation to determine the current fair market value of your company. • Will the current value of your company be enough to meet your Financial Transition Goal? • Do you have a Business Value Gap?	Your CPA or a Business Valuation specialist
	Assemble your Collaborative Team of Transition Advisors. Choose a Lead Advisor or Chief Transition Officer.	The specific advisors you will work with will depend on your specific situation and Transition Goals.
Business Continuation Process:	Inform your employees, customers, vendors, etc. that you are planning to transition out of your company, and that you have a comprehensive plan for how this will happen.	A Management Consultant
	Actively involve your employees in preparing for the Business Transition Process.	A Management Consultant

Figure 8-C

Creating Your Business Transition Plan

Stage Three of the Transition Process

The Four Transition Tracks	Activities	Transition Advisors Who Can Help You
Personal Transition Process:	Ongoing	
Personal Financial Planning:	Ongoing	
Business Transition Process:	Meet regularly with your Lead Advisor/Chief Transition Officer and your Transition Advisory Team to develop and refine your Business Transition Strategic Plan.	The specific advisors you work with will depend on your specific situation and Transition Goals.
	If the current value of your company is not enough to meet your Financial Transition Goal, you will need to create a strategy for improving your business and increasing its value as part of your Business Transition Plan.	A Management Consultant
Business Continuation Process:	Keep your employees motivated and committed to the company during the transition process.	A Management Consultant

Figure 8-D

Implementing Your Business Transition Plan

Stage Four of the Transition Process

The Four Transition Tracks	Activities	Transition Advisors Who Can Help You
Personal Transition Process:	Ongoing	
Personal Financial Planning:	Ongoing	
Business Transition Process:	Determine changes and improvements needed so your company will meet your financial goals and be more attractive to a new owner. Implement these changes. Actively involve your employees in improving your company's value.	A Management Consultant
	Begin the process of preparing and training the potential new owner/s.	A Management Consultant
	OR Begin the process of looking for an outside buyer for the company.	A Business Intermediary can help find an outside buyer.
	When you are ready to transfer your company to the new owner, do business tax planning to minimize business taxes through the transfer.	Your CPA
Business Continuation Process:	Ongoing	

Figure 8-E

Negotiating the Deal

Stage Five of the Transition Process

The Four Transition Tracks	Activities	Transition Advisors Who Can Help You
Personal Transition Process:	Decide if you will make a clean break, or how long you will stay on to help the new owner.	
Personal Financial Planning:	Negotiate how you will be paid. Will you get the full amount for your company up-front? Or will you receive future payments from the company's future profits under the new owner?	If this is an internal transfer, or if you are selling your company directly to an outside buyer, your CPA, a Business Attorney or an M&A Attorney can help you with the negotiations. If you are working with a Business Intermediary to sell to an outside buyer, the Business Intermediary will help you negotiate the sale.
Business Transition Process:	Negotiate the deal.	If this is an internal transfer, or if you are selling your company directly to an outside buyer, your CPA, a Business Attorney or an M&A Attorney can help you with the negotiations. If you are working with a Business Intermediary to sell to an outside buyer, the Business Intermediary will help you negotiate the sale.
Business Continuation Process:	Transfer your company to the new owner.	

MOVE ON TO YOUR NEW LIFE!

How You – the Owner – Should Be Involved in Creating and Implementing Your Business Transition Strategic Plan

As the owner of your company, you have key decisions to make and key actions to take in order to assure your successful business transition. The rest of this book explains these key decisions and actions and how to successfully achieve their implementation.

Chapter 9 explains how to design the personal, business and financial goals you want to achieve through the Business Transition Process; why these "outcome goals" are central to choosing the best new owner for your company; and helps you analyze a range of options so you can determine which strategy for finding new ownership will best meet your personal, business and financial goals.

Chapter 10 describes key "process goals" you need to consider in your Business Transition Strategic Plan, and how to prepare your company for the Business Transition Process.

Chapter 11 explains how to assemble and work most effectively with a Collaborative Team of Transition Advisors in creating and implementing your Business Transition Strategic Plan.

Chapter 12 describes how a Transition Planning Consultant can help you work with both the Head and Heart issues of the Transition Process to become mentally and emotionally prepared, design your Personal and Business Transition Goals and create your unique Personal Transition Plan for a new life you can't wait to live.

CHAPTER 9

Expanding Your Thinking about Your Options for New Ownership

Who would be the best new owner for your company?

Maybe you already have someone in mind to take over – or maybe you have no idea who the best new owner might be or how to find him.

Maybe you assume that you will have to sell your company to another firm or to outside investors, when the best candidate may actually be someone in your family or from among your employees (an "internal transfer"). Or maybe you've decided that your children will take over, but they may be uninterested or unqualified, and seeking an outside buyer (an "external" transfer) may actually be your best choice. (Your plan for who will become the new owner and how they will move into ownership is also called a "succession plan," especially when the transition takes place internally.)

This chapter helps you expand your thinking about new ownership for your company. It looks at both the "objective" issues, such as the available options, qualifications of the new owner and various financing arrangements, as well as the personal and emotional issues involved in deciding on and finding the best new owner for your company.

Seven Options for New Ownership

- Your partner/s or co-owner/s
- A family member or members (your child/ren, sibling/s, or other relatives)
- Key employee/s
- All your employees
- Selling directly to an outside buyer
- Using a business intermediary to sell to an outside buyer
- Private equity recapitalization (temporary ownership by outside investors)

There are also other ways to transfer your company to new ownership, but the seven options listed here are among those that owners most frequently use.

Which of these seven options for new ownership is best for your situation and your company? To answer this question you first need to think about the goals you want to achieve through the Business Transition Process. We will begin by considering your Personal Outcome Goals, your Outcome Goals for your Company and your Legacy Goals.

Your Personal Outcome Goals (for yourself and your family)

Your Personal Outcome Goals are your Core Transition Goals – your transition "bottom line." Your overriding priority is to achieve these Core Transition Goals through the Business Transition Process. All other goals are secondary.

Your Personal Outcome Goals are your Core Transition Goals – your transition "bottom line." Your overriding priority is to achieve these Personal Outcome Goals through the Business Transition Process.

Your Personal Outcome Goals will include the following:

- Time: Your desired Departure Date.

- Money: Your Financial Transition Goal – this is the amount of money you will need from your company to support your new life, along with any additional future financial goals you may have. (See below.)

- Assuring a successful future for the company after you have left. (This is an essential goal if you are counting on deferred future payments from the new owners to support your new life.)

Think about and write down the Personal Outcome Goals (your Core Transition Goals for yourself and your family) that you want to achieve through the Business Transition Process.

Your Financial Transition Goal

How much money will you need for your new life? You determine this by designing a comprehensive plan for the new life you want to live, then have your Personal Financial Planner or Wealth Management Advisor determine how much money you will need for this future and if your current assets and investments will be enough to support your future plans. (Refer back to Chapter 6.)

You may have other personal financial goals in addition to supporting the new life you want to move into. For example, you may also want to help pay for your grandchildren's college tuition, set up a philanthropic foundation, or you may have other goals you will want to finance after you have left the company.

Once you know how much money you want or need for your future life, you and your advisor can determine how much money you will need from your company to help pay for your future needs.

If it turns out that you already have enough money from your personal assets and investments to cover your future needs, so that your future well-being is not dependent on money from your company, then – Lucky You! – you will have considerable flexibility in how you conduct your Business Transition Process, including greater flexibility in choosing the best new owner for your company.

However, you and your advisor may discover that you have a Personal Financial Gap and you will need money from your company to help pay for your future life. The amount of money you want from your company by transferring it to new owners is your "Financial Transition Goal." (See Figure 9-A.)

The amount of money you will need to support your future life (or to support other future plans) creates a baseline for your Financial Transition Goal – i.e. this is the minimum amount you will want to aim for from your company.

You might decide that your desired Financial Transition Goal should be higher than this baseline. For various reasons, you might even decide that your priority is to get the most money possible from your company, or to get the most money possible, up-front, through the process of transferring it to new owners, with other goals or other non-financial considerations of secondary or minimal importance.

On the other hand, various non-financial issues or other longer-term considerations might be important enough to you that you will not seek the maximum amount of money possible from the company. Instead, you can aim for your minimum – baseline – goal, with the financial flexibility that allows you to make other goals for your company or your future life a priority. (For more about your Financial Transition Goal, flexibility and negotiating tradeoffs, see "Your Outcome Goals for your Company" and "Your Legacy Goals," below.)

Figure 9-A

Your Financial Transition Goal

1. Do you have a Personal Financial Gap? **How much money will you need from your company** to support your future life and any other future financial plans? (Refer back to Figure 6-C.)
   - This is your **Financial Transition Goal**.

2. Do a Business Valuation for your company.
   - How much is your company worth **now**?

3. Will the current value of your company be enough to meet your Financial Transition Goal?
   - If yes, go ahead with looking for a new owner for your company.
   - If the current value of your company is <u>not</u> enough to meet your Financial Transition Goal, this means that you have a **Business Value Gap**.

4. Before you are ready to transfer your company to new ownership, you will first have to **increase the value of your company** so it can bring you enough money to meet your Financial Transition Goal. (See Chapter 10.)

Outcome Goals for Your Company

The outcome goals you have for your company are of importance not only to you personally, but will also impact the lives and future well-being of your employees or even your larger community. Examples of outcome goals for your company might include:

- Keeping the company in your local community
- Continue providing local employment through the company
- Taking care of long-time employees
- Assuring your customers continued high-quality products and services
- Seeing new products that you have been working on come to fruition

These are goals that you would like the company to continue after you have left – goals that you feel strongly about, and with good reason. But in order to achieve your Core Transition Goals (see above, "Your Personal Outcome Goals"), some of your goals for your company may have to be negotiable. If you have flexibility in your Core Goals, especially in your Financial Transition Goal, you will have more freedom to find a new owner who values these goals for your company as much as you do.

Think about and write down the Outcome Goals for Your Company that you want to achieve through the Business Transition Process.

Your Legacy Goals

In this context, "Legacy" refers not to your financial legacy, but to the unique characteristics or activities that you created in your company and that you hope will be continued by the new owner. Examples of Legacy Goals:

- Continuing a corporate culture that encourages employees' innovation and promotes their career development
- Continuing the company's community or philanthropic involvement
- Wanting to be remembered as "the founder of the company" after you've moved on

Legacy Goals depend on the owner's unique interests, abilities, management style and values, which is why they are the most difficult to assure through the Business Transition Process. The new owner may decide to continue your Legacy Goals in a different way – for example, choosing to donate some of the company's profits to a health charity instead of supporting Little League. Or they may not continue these practices at all. Even though you have deep emotional attachments to your Legacy Goals, you may have to let them go in order to secure your higher priority goals. If you have flexibility in your Core Goals, especially in your Financial Transition Goal, you will have more freedom to find a new owner who values your Legacy Goals as much as you do.

Think about and write down any Legacy Goals for your company that you would like to achieve through the Business Transition Process.

How much money is your company worth?

In order to design a strategic plan for meeting your financial goals through the Business Transition Process, you have to know how much money your company is worth now.

You get this information by having a professional business valuation done for your company. This can be done by your CPA, by a business valuation specialist, or by a member of an M&A firm.

Fair market value: The business valuation will tell you the current fair market value of your business. (You need this information not only to determine if the current value of your company will allow you to meet your financial goals, but also because some methods for transferring your company to new owners, such as succession in the family or creating an ESOP, are based on your company's fair market value.)

But doing a business valuation and learning your company's fair market value are only the first steps. Your strategic plan should also consider two other ways of determining your company's value:

Synergy value: Your company's synergy value refers to how much your company is worth to an outside owner, especially to another company that sees value in your company for their needs and situation. In other words, your company's synergy value is not how much you think your company is worth, but how much an interested buyer thinks it is worth for their purposes.

(The value an outside buyer sees in your company can be based on widely varying criteria. For example, one buyer may want to purchase your company because your product line can help expand their existing customer base; another buyer may want your company because they have plans for reusing your company's physical plant or real estate for their own purposes; while a third buyer may want to purchase your company because they appreciate the quality of your product and employees and want to continue running a company with such an excellent reputation.)

Potential future value: The business valuation tells you how much your company is worth now. But a key part of your strategic plan may be to improve your company's operations and increase its bottom line before you are ready to pass it on to a new owner. (Chapter 10 says more about why and how to increase your company's value before you leave.)

How will you transition out of your company?

In order to create a Business Transition Process that meets your personal, business and financial goals, you need to think about how you want to leave your company. This includes both the timing and financial arrangements that will be part of your strategic plan and in your contract with the new owner.

How will you transition out of your company? – Timing

Making a clean break: When you and the new owner are ready to negotiate your deal, you may be able to get all your money up-front, make a clean break from the company and quickly move on to your new life.

Staying on temporarily: For various reasons, you may need to spend some time working with – or for – the new owner, helping them get up to speed before you can actually leave. An important emotional consideration when agreeing to stay on and help the new owner is that you will have to temporarily shift your mindset and identity, from being owner of your company, to becoming an employee of the new owner for a specific period of time. Many owners have done this, but it can be an emotionally difficult transition.

Another key consideration is to be clear about how long you will be working for the new owner. Remember – your ultimate goal is to move on to your new life. You don't want to be stuck working for the new owner any longer than necessary.

How will you transition out of your company? – Financial arrangements

There are numerous technical, legal and financial aspects that you and your advisors need to work through as part of your contract with the new owner – including tax issues, how you will be paid (in cash, in stock, by promissory note, etc.), and how the deal will be financed.

In addition to these transactional aspects, you also need to think about how your financial arrangements with the new owner will affect your quality of life – during the transition process and also after you have left. Here are several options and how each will affect your life.

Getting paid up-front: Getting all your money up-front when you leave is often the most desirable alternative. You know you have achieved your financial goal, you don't have to worry about what happens to the company after you leave and you are free to move on to your new life.

Deferred future payments: The person/s you have decided on as the best new owner for your company may not have the capital available to pay you up-front for the full price of the company. One strategy that many owners choose is to contract to be paid by the new owner later on – out of the new owner's expected future profits – over a future period of time ("deferred future payments").

There are many ways to structure a deal based on receiving deferred future payments. Your professional financial advisors are essential for helping you design and negotiate this agreement to achieve the best terms for you. Issues to be considered include: will you get any money up front, the amount of each future payment, how often you will be paid, and for how long these future payments will be continued.

Note: Some professional advisors specialize in working with new owners who lack capital up-front, to help them design self-financing future payment plans through which the employees or other new owners are able to pay the owner over time from the company's future profits.

Relying on deferred future payments to fund your future lifestyle means that your ability to enjoy your new life depends on the new owner's future success. What will you do if under the new owner the company does poorly and the new owner is unable to pay you the expected future payments? Your business transition strategy should include ways for dealing with this possibility. For example:

- Your transition strategy should include methods for preparing the new owner to be successful (see Chapter 10).

- If you have to depend on deferred future payments from the new owner and you are not sure that they will be successful, you will need to build a contingency plan into your contract with the new owner for how you will take back ownership and control of the business if the new owner fails. This means that if the new owner fails, you may have to leave your new life and go back to work!

Seven Options for New Ownership

Here are some of the major options for new ownership:

- Your partner or co-owner
- A family member or members (your child/ren, sibling/s, or other relatives)
- A key employee (or key employees)
- All your employees
- Selling directly to an outside buyer (outside buyers are also called "third-party buyers")
- Using a business intermediary (such as an investment banker or M&A firm) to sell to an outside buyer/third-party buyer
- Private equity recapitalization (temporary ownership by outside investors)

There are other ways to transfer your company to new ownership, but these seven options are among those that owners most frequently use. The rest of this chapter explains each of these options, describes general benefits and drawbacks of each, helps you consider which options are feasible for your situation, and shows you how to analyze the advantages and disadvantages of each option for your specific situation so you can choose the best new owner for your company.

"Objective" Benefits and Drawbacks of the Seven Options

First, here are some well-known facts that can give you a general idea of what each of these seven options for new ownership can offer you and your company.

- Family transfers can be deeply emotional, may stir up family problems and have a high rate of failure. In fact, about 70% of family-owned businesses fail after transfer to the next generation.

Even though family succession may seem like an obvious choice, another option may actually be better for you, your family and your company.

- Partners and employees are already familiar with the company. But they may need some training, and/or may not have available capital up-front. They may need outside assistance with financing, or you may have to negotiate a deferred future payment plan with them.

- Outside buyer: You can get the highest price for your company from an outside buyer (because of your company's synergy value for <u>their</u> needs), but an outside buyer may not want to continue your company goals or your legacy goals.

- Going through a business intermediary: They will do the work of finding the new buyer, while you can focus on running the company.

- Private equity group recapitalization: You may have to switch from being an owner to becoming an employee for a while.

Consider the Feasibility of Each Option for Your Specific Situation

This section discusses some of the specific issues related to each of these seven options for new ownership, to help you consider whether or not this option is feasible for your personal goals and your company's situation.

1. <u>Selling your company to your Partner/s or Co-owner/s</u>

If you have a business partner or co-owner who wants to take over and run the company, this may be the most preferable option. Your partner/co-owner is already familiar with the company, and may need little or no training to take over. If your partner/co-owner is interested, do they have the capital available to pay you up-front, or will they need to find a financing source so they can buy you out ?

If your partner/co-owner is in your age-range, they may also be thinking about leaving the company and moving on to a new life, which means you will have to consider other options for new ownership.

2. <u>Passing your company on to a Family Member or Members (such as your child/ren, sibling/s, or other relatives)</u>

This is the first option that many owners automatically think of when planning to leave – but it may or may not be the best choice.

If you have a family member(s) who wants to own and run the company, and if this relative (or group of relatives) has already spent time working in the company, they may already be familiar with the business and qualified to take over. You may have to train the new owner in some additional skills needed to run the company. The competence and experience of the family member(s) replacing you as owner will determine how much time will be needed to prepare them to take over.

Your family member/s may not have the capital to pay you outright for your company, which means that you will have to depend on deferred future payments from them after they have become the new owner. You may also want to include in your contract a contingency plan for how you can take back ownership and control of the business if the new owner fails.

Perhaps the biggest drawback is that family succession can be fraught with emotional issues. Rivalry among siblings, personal animosities, conflicts and many other emotionally intense and potentially disruptive issues that can harm both the family and the business often erupt during the process of trying to pass the company on to other family members, or after the new owners have taken over. That's why organizations that specialize in helping transfer businesses within the family often recommend psychological counseling for the family members as an essential part of the family business transition!

Be sure that the family members who will take over your company are both qualified and emotionally compatible. Learn about the unique issues involved in transferring a business within the family, so you and your successors will be prepared for these potential problems.

Note: A transition advisory team helping with family succession needs a unique skill set. In a multi-generational transition, the team's focus should be on mobilizing the various family members to be intelligent stewards of the business and using the company as a vehicle for unifying the family. Their goals should be both to develop the business under its current owners, and develop good governance and a family legacy into the third, fourth and fifth generations.

For more information about transferring the business within the family, see The Family Firm Institute, www.ffi.org .

3. Selling your company to a Key Employee or Key Employees (such as to your Management Team)

You may have a key employee, or a group of key employees, such as your management team, who are interested in owning and running the company. Your key employees are already familiar with the company and industry issues, and may need only a little training to take over. However, they may not have the capital to pay you up-front for your company, which means they will either need to arrange financing for themselves, or arrange to pay you through deferred future payments out of their future profits.

4. Selling your company to all your employees

Your employees can become the owners of your company by purchasing shares of stock directly, by being given a grant of shares or options to buy shares, by being given equity rights that translate into the value of shares, by transferring through some kind of employee trust, or by creating a worker-owned cooperative. Various kinds of employee ownership come with varying rights to a governance role in the company.

4.a Creating an ESOP (Employee Stock Ownership Plan)

An ESOP is a retirement plan through which employees gain financial ownership of the company, but do not have a governance role. Creating an ESOP allows you to have significant internal control over the transaction, and can take less time to implement compared to an external sale. With an ESOP, the owner can decide if they want to sell all the ownership to the employees, or if they want to transition ownership gradually over time.

ESOPs are a strategy through which an owner gradually begins the process of converting their closely-held ownership of the company into liquid capital. It is also a good way to vest employees in the company and boost morale. The opportunity to share in company growth and performance gives employees a sense of ownership and encourages their contributions to the success of the company.

ESOPs also have a number of attractive tax and investment benefits. The loan used to finance the ESOP transaction is effectively repaid by the company with pre-tax dollars. On the negative side, creating an ESOP can be quite complex, since it requires understanding of a unique combination of fields such as valuation, business transaction dynamics, tax law and regulatory compliance under ERISA. An ESOP also requires ongoing administrative costs, including annual valuation, plan administration and trustee fees.

For more information about ESOPs, consult an ESOP Attorney or contact the ESOP Association, www.esopassociation.org or the ICA Group, www.ica-group.org .

4.b Creating an employee-owned and run company

If you have a strong internal culture of dedicated and competent employees, creating an employee-owned and run company – also known as a worker-owned company – may be a good option for you. In this strategy, the workers may show interest in buying and maintaining the company, raising equity either from outside or from among themselves, so they can take over when the current owner retires.

In addition to the need for financing, creating a worker-owner company also requires training the employees in self-management methods and other business issues so they can continue the company successfully.

For more information about how to start a worker-owned cooperative, see the US Federation of Worker Cooperatives, www.usworker.coop ; the International Cooperative Alliance, www.ica.coop ; the National Cooperative Business Association, www.ncba.coop ; the National Cooperative Bank, www.ncb.coop ; or the ICA Group, www.ica-group.org .

5. Selling directly to an Outside Buyer (to another individual, or to another company)

If an interested individual or company has already approached you about buying your company, you may simply decide to sell it to them. Or because of your familiarity with your industry, you may know of another company (or other companies) that would be interested in purchasing your company, and you may decide to try selling it yourself.

If the potential buyer is already in your industry, they are familiar with the business issues that affect your company. Since your company may have synergy value for another company, selling to another company may bring you the highest financial return, compared with all other options for new ownership.

However, another company who takes over may or may not be willing to continue your goals for your company. They may have another agenda. You may have to consider trade-offs when selling to another company.

If you choose to sell your company yourself, your CPA, your Business Attorney or an M&A Attorney can help you negotiate the deal.

6. Using a Business Intermediary to sell your company to an outside buyer

If you don't have a potential new owner already lined up, going to a Business Intermediary experienced in finding and negotiating with buyers may be your best option. The intermediary focuses their energy and expertise on finding the best new owner for your company, while you can stay focused on preparing your company for transition and keeping it running successfully day-to-day.

Another benefit of going through a Business Intermediary is that they often analyze the strengths and weaknesses of your company, and recommend changes and improvements you should make in order to make your company more attractive and have more value to a new owner. (For more about how to increase the value of your company, see Chapter 10.)

Because the Business Intermediary wants to find a buyer who will pay you the highest price for your company, they can use methods such as a controlled auction among several potential buyers to get you the highest price.

Time is also a key consideration when using a Business Intermediary to find an outside buyer for your company. The time it takes to find and negotiate with a desirable outside buyer will depend on the market, economic conditions and the unique value of your company. The process may happen very quickly – or it could take several years to find a suitable outside buyer.

There are three types of Business Intermediaries: Business Brokers, Investment Bankers and M&A firms. Business Brokers usually represent lower-priced companies, while M&A firms and Investment Bankers work with high-end companies.

A Business Broker helps an owner determine an appropriate price for their company, then creates a marketing strategy (although this may simply be to list the availability of the firm), interviews and shows the business to qualified buyers, helps the owner decide on the best offer, then negotiates the deal.

Investment Bankers typically represent financial institutions. They help buy or sell companies, raise capital, and also help companies issue stock for initial public stock offering. They can help in recruiting attorneys or accountants with experience commensurate with a large transaction. They prepare marketing documents to arouse buyers' interest; initiate contact with potential buyers and assist in negotiating the business and financing issues in the sale agreement.

M&A firms are similar to Investment Bankers in that they introduce owners to strategic buyers who often place the highest value on your company, as well as financial buyers such as private equity firms that have significant liquidity available to invest in companies. M&A firms will also help companies raise capital for internal growth as well as for buying other companies. Some M&A firms are advisors only, and do not offer financing.

7. <u>Private Equity Recapitalization (temporary ownership by outside investors)</u>

One way to obtain enough wealth from your company to support your future life is to grow the company as a transition strategy. This is where Private Equity Recapitalization can be helpful.

There are many firms that offer capital to owners in exchange for a substantial ownership stake (usually 75%-80%). These firms are almost always groups of investors, hence the name Private Equity Groups (PE for short). The PEs represent investors who are seeking financial return by investing in a portfolio of companies. This means that a PE who has invested in your firm has no emotional attachment to your company, but sees it as part of a portfolio of investments.

If you accept an offer from a PE, you will likely receive capital in a mix of debt and equity. Much of your equity interest in the company will be replaced by the equity of the PE, but you will retain a small portion of the company to incent you to keep growing the business. The PE will give you a 3-5 year contract, during which time you are in essence working as their employee. Because the PE wants to grow your company's value at 20% per year, they may institute many controls over financial and other decisions to "professionalize" your company's operations and assure increased profitability. The benefit is that you could double your company's earnings in 4-5 years, vastly increasing the valuation of your shares.

In 5 to 7 years the PE will put your company up for sale. At this point you can sell out entirely, find a new PE to replace the former one, or you will have the option of buying back your company if you wish (known as "getting a second bite of the apple").

Analyze How the Benefits and Drawbacks of Each Option for New Ownership Apply to Your Specific Situation

Below are 11 questions to help you analyze each of the Seven Options for New Ownership, to help you determine how well each option meets your personal, business and financial goals.

- You can use these 11 questions to help you make your decision if you don't have a choice in mind yet for who the best new owner would be, and you want to explore all potential options. (To do this, take 7 pieces of paper and write a different option for new ownership at the top of each page. Then for each option, answer the 11 questions below.)

- You should also use these questions if you already have a specific choice in mind, and you want to appraise its advantages and disadvantages objectively and be able to compare it objectively with other potential options.

1. Are you open to considering this option?
2. Are they <u>interested</u> in becoming the new owner? If you don't know, how can you find out?
3. Are they <u>capable/qualified</u> to become the new owner?
4. Do they have the experience and abilities to take over as new owner <u>right now</u>?
5. Do they need to be <u>prepared or trained</u> in order to run the company successfully? If they need training, <u>how much time will it take</u> to get them up to speed?
6. Are they <u>willing to pay</u> you the amount of money you want for the company (your Financial Transition Goal)?
7. Do they have the <u>capital available now</u> to pay you the money you want for the company?
8. If they do not have the capital available now, can they <u>develop a source of financing</u> so they can pay you now?
9. OR – Are you willing to <u>create a deferred future payment agreement</u> with the new owner, through which they will pay you over time from the company's future profits?

10. Will you be required to spend time working with – or working for – the new owner, to help get them up to speed before you leave? If yes, how much time will you need to spend working with/for the new owner before you can leave?

11. If you are depending on deferred future payments from the new owner – but you are not sure that they will be able to run the company successfully – are you willing to create a "fall-back" arrangement with them, so you can take back ownership of the company and put it back on track, if needed? (This means that if the new owner doesn't work out, you may have to quit your new lifestyle and go back to work!)

Deciding on the Best New Owner for Your Company

Reflect on how you answered these 11 questions for each option, and consider how each of these Seven Options for New Ownership interfaces with your Core Transition Goals, and with your other personal, business or financial goals, for yourself and for your company.

> Which of these options for new ownership is best for you – personally, emotionally, financially, in terms of time?
>
> Which other options are worth considering?

If more than one of these options seems viable for you, you can develop a prioritized list of your best possible options for new ownership.

Designing Your Business Transition Goals

This chapter has helped you think about the personal, business and financial goals that you want to achieve through transitioning your company to new ownership, and has helped you do a preliminary analysis of who might be the best new owner for your company or what your best transition strategy might be. Figure 9-B will help you focus on and summarize these key transition goals.

Your responses to the questions in Figure 9-B will be central to the creation of your Business Transition Strategic Plan (see Chapter 11).

Figure 9-B

My Business Transition Goals

1. What **Personal Outcome Goals** do I want to achieve for my family and myself through the business transition? • Time: My desired Departure Date. • Money: The amount of money I want to receive through transitioning my company to new owners (my Financial Transition Goal). • Assuring that the company continues successfully after I have left. These are my Core Transition Goals. They take priority over all other transition goals.	
2. What **Outcome Goals for my Company** do I want to achieve through the business transition?	
3. What **Legacy Goals** do I want to achieve through the business transition?	
4. Who would be **the best new owner** for my company? • What would be the best strategy for finding new ownership?	

CHAPTER 10

Expanding Your Thinking about the Future of Your Company

After 26 years of running their pest control business, Mr. and Mrs. Q were ready to retire. They wanted to sell the company to their two sons, who had been involved in the business since their late teens. The owners hired Kevin H., a management consultant, to help them and their sons design a deal that would work for everyone involved. The two sons would buy the company's stock, not for cash, but by giving their parents a note for 100% of the sale price, with the expectation that the sons would pay their parents $8,000 each month to help meet their retirement expenses. Since this monthly payment of $8,000 represents 60% of the income Mr. and Mrs. Q are counting on to fund their retirement, they are relying heavily on their sons' ability to run the company together successfully and to generate sufficient cash flow to meet the monthly $8,000 obligation on a timely and consistent basis.

The consultant's job was to make sure that the two sons were ready to take over and would be successful once the sale was finalized and the parents retired. The plan Kevin created includes: developing a solid stockholders' agreement that defines how the two sons will jointly govern the company and deals with potential contingencies that might arise; a job description for each son which defines the role each will play in the day-to-day running of the company; doing a "gap analysis" of what skills and abilities the two sons currently possess and what skills they will need to develop before taking on their new roles; establishing individual succession plans for each son, based on the gap analysis; and developing a 5-year business plan for the two sons, to provide them with a road map for success.

In this story and the others in this chapter, the names and identifying characteristics of those involved have been changed to protect their privacy.

You know that you need to prepare yourself mentally and emotionally for the Transition Process.

As the above story shows, you may also need to prepare the new owners to be successful in their new roles.

You also need to prepare your company for a successful transition process.

Transitioning your company to new ownership not only opens up the opportunity for you to do something new with your life, but also gives your company the opportunity to change and grow. New ownership can bring new ideas and new ways of doing things into your company. And the process of preparing your company for new ownership can help you recognize and deal with its weaknesses and build on its strengths, improving operations and increasing the bottom line.

Chapter 9 explained how to design the outcome goals you want to achieve through the Business Transition Process. This chapter focuses on your process goals – that is, the goals you will need to accomplish during each step of the Business Transition Process in order to transition successfully. Process goals are usually transactional issues, but many of them also have emotional aspects.

Fifteen Questions to Help You Accomplish the Process Goals Essential for Your Business Transition

1. Record-Keeping: Are all of my company's legal documents and financial records in order and up to date?

2. Business Valuation: How much money is my company worth right now?

3. Business Value Gap: Do I have a "Business Value Gap?" Is the current value of my company enough to provide me with the money I will need to support the new life I have planned?

4. Business Readiness: Is my company ready now to transfer to new owners?

4.a. Do I first need to increase the value of my company, so it will be attractive to new owners, and its transfer will meet my financial needs?

4.b. Do I need to improve my company's operations so it will have more value and be more likely to remain successful after I have left?

4.c. Do I need to grow my business so it will have more value when I transfer it to new owners?

5. Business Continuity Plan: Have I created a Business Continuity Plan for who will run the company in the event of my sudden or unexpected departure?

6. A New Head of Operations: Should I create the formal position of Chief Operations Officer (or General Manager) for the company, and train or hire a qualified individual to be in charge of the company's day-to-day operations?

7. Options for New Ownership: Have I explored all my options for a new owner/s for my company, and considered the benefits and drawbacks of each option?

8. Best New Owner: Have I decided on who would be the best new owner for my company?

9. New-Owner Readiness: Is the best choice for new owner ready now to take on the ownership role? Do I need to prepare and train them for ownership?

10. OR Finding a New Owner: Do I need to find a new owner for my company? Do I have a strategy for finding the best new owner?

11. Motivating Employees: Do I have a strategy for keeping my employees motivated and committed to improving the company during the transition process?

12. Continuing My Legacy: What values and characteristics would I like continued in the company when it is transferred to new owners? Do I have a strategy for continuing my legacy after I have left?

13. Negotiating the Deal: Do I have a strategy for negotiating with the new owner so I can leave on my terms (selling price, timing of payouts, time when I will leave, etc.)?

14. Minimizing Business Taxes: Do I have a strategy for minimizing my business taxes during the Business Transition Process? Do I have professional advisors who can help me with this priority?

15. Collaborative Advisory Team:
    - 15.a. Am I aware of the types of professional advisors who can help me with the various aspects of designing and implementing my business transition strategy?
    - 15.b. Do I know how to assemble, and how to work most effectively with a Collaborative Team of Transition Advisors, so they can most successfully help me achieve my personal, business and financial goals through the transition process?

The next sections explain more fully how and why you need to answer each of these 15 questions.

Record-keeping

Before you even think about transferring your company to a new owner, you first have to get all your company's legal documents and financial records up to date. Talk to your CPA and business attorney about your intention to transfer the company to new owners, and ask them to help you prepare for this transition.

Business Valuation

In order to design a strategic plan for meeting your personal, business and financial goals through the Business Transition Process, you have to know what your company is worth now (its current fair market value). You get this information by having a professional business valuation done for your company. This information is crucial not only as a starting point for planning the rest of your business transition strategy, but also because some methods for transferring your company to new owners, such as succession in the family or creating an ESOP, are based on your company's fair market value. A business valuation can be done by your CPA or by a business valuation specialist.

Business Value Gap

When you know the current value of your company, you can determine if your business can provide you with the money you will need to support your future lifestyle, or if you have a Business Value Gap (refer back to Figure 9-A).

Business Readiness (Increasing the value of your company)

If you have a Business Value Gap, this means that your company is not ready to be transferred to a new owner. In order to fill this gap, you need to increase the value of your company so it can provide you with the money you will need for your future life by the time you leave. (The second half of this chapter provides more information about why and how to improve the value of your business.)

A Business Continuity Plan and a New Head of Operations

What would happen to the company if you suddenly became seriously ill, disabled or died? Who would run the company if you were no longer there? These questions are crucial not only for you, but also for the future well-being of your family.

This issue is especially important if you are spending much of your time at work dealing with your company's day-to-day operations – or if you do not have a formal Chief Operating Officer or General Manager who is officially in charge of day-to-day operations.

If you are doing most of the work of a COO now in addition to all your other responsibilities, you and your company can benefit significantly by creating a formal COO position and finding or training a qualified person to fill this key management position. Furthermore, in the event of your unexpected departure, your COO will be able to keep the company running day-to-day while your heirs or co-owner decide what to do next. A management consultant can help you determine the job description, responsibilities and qualifications for an effective COO.

A Business Continuity Plan is also essential for designating what will happen to your company if you leave unexpectedly. If you have not already done so, consult with your business attorney about creating this plan for you.

Analyzing Your Options for New Ownership and Deciding on Who Would Be the Best New Owner for Your Company

Refer back to Chapter 9.

New-Owner Readiness

The person/s who you decided would be the best new owner may need to be trained or otherwise prepared in order to take over the ownership role and run the company successfully. A professional management consultant can help you determine what skills your potential new owner needs to acquire, and can help you create an appropriate training program.

Finding a New Owner

Chapter 9 also explained strategies you can use to find the best new owner for your company.

Motivating Your Employees to Support the Business Transition Process

When your employees learn that you are planning to leave the company and transfer it to a new owner, they may – understandably – be concerned about their own futures, and might even think about leaving the company in order to find more secure positions. You do not want to lose employees now – you certainly don't want to lose your key employees, whose contributions are so vital to your company's success.

Keeping your employees committed to the company and involved in supporting the Business Transition Process has both emotional and transactional components. At the emotional level, you want to assure your employees that you take their concerns very seriously and your plan for leaving will include measures to assure their continued employment and good treatment. If you plan to transfer the company internally to someone your employees already know, such as a partner/co-owner, a family member or to a key employee/s, your employees may feel more secure because they are already familiar with the intended new owner.

Your planned transition may feel less secure to your employees if you are intending to sell to an outside buyer. Everyone knows "horror stories" about a company which was sold to a new owner, and the new owner fired the current employees or closed the existing plant and moved the firm to a new location (to another city, state, or even across the ocean). Whether or not this could happen to your company will depend in part on the product or service you are providing, and if it can be provided effectively only from your current location.

It's important to be candid with your employees about your future plans, to listen to their concerns, and if possible, include their concerns in your negotiations with the new owner. There are also a variety of financial methods and systems for motivating your employees to stay loyal to the company and helping you during the Business Transition Process. A management consultant can help you design financial incentive packages that will encourage your employees to stay committed to the company and the Business Transition Process.

Continuing Your Legacy

Chapter 9 discussed what legacy you might want to see continued in the company after you have left, and how you might achieve this goal.

Minimizing Business Taxes

You will want to work with your professional advisors to help you design and negotiate the best deal with the new owner and minimize taxes as you transition your company to new owners.

Business tax planning is best done when you first form your company: C-Corp, S-Corp and LLC are some of the most popular kinds. But now is not too late to do business tax planning. Take some time to discuss options with your CPA and Business Attorney. You will at least be better informed before you actually transfer your business.

You need to keep all tax planning advice in alignment with your personal goals. For example, if advisors suggest a strategy that they say will reduce your taxes and transfer the wealth in your company tax-free to your children, beware of the issues involved. You may end up bringing family problems into the business.

Another issue that may arise is whether your current CPA firm can handle the tax issues related to the transfer of your business. If they are not familiar with the transfer process (especially larger transactions in the many millions of dollars), you should seek referrals to other CPA firms. You are not abandoning your current CPA, just adding to your "Dream Team" of advisors (see Chapter 11).

Lastly, you need to find tax advisors who can put your needs ahead of their egos. These advisors are used to being "the experts." But your business and personal futures are at stake. Push hard for what you want, ask tough questions and be prepared to make tough decisions.

Negotiating the Deal

If the deal is an internal transfer (for example, transitioning the company to your partner/co-owner, to another member of your family, or to your employees), or if you personally are selling your company directly to an outside buyer, your CPA, a Business Attorney or an M&A Attorney can help you design and negotiate the deal.

If you are working with a Business Intermediary to sell your company to an outside buyer, the Intermediary will help you negotiate the deal.

Improving the Value of Your Company as a Key Piece of Your Transition Strategy

Mr. and Mrs. R ran a commercial interior design business for about 20 years. By their early sixties they knew that they wanted to retire in five years, but had no specific plan for how to do so. After consulting with their personal financial planner to determine their future financial needs and how much money they would need from selling the business to fund their retirement, they began working with Kyle H., a management consultant, to help them design and implement their business transition strategy.

Kyle H. recommended a professional appraisal of the current value of the business, which revealed that there was a significant gap between its current value and the owners' desired sale price. Kyle then put together a 5-year plan with specific revenue, cash flow and net income goals in order to increase the company's value. During the process of implementing this strategy, Mr. and Mrs. R learned that two key employees were interested in buying the company. Now that they have increased the value of their company based on their plan for improved sales and earnings, the owners and their key employees have begun a succession and buyout financing plan.

Mr. S owned an $8 million dollar manufacturing company with about 40 employees that produced tooling for its client companies. Although it had top of the line equipment and a pristine factory, there were bottlenecks in the work flow. Mr. S hired Henry W., a management consultant, to improve his company's performance.

After analyzing the company's operations, Henry determined that the company was inefficient because of poor systems, poor work flow and poor management skills. The key staff agreed with the consultant's conclusions and together they considered and evaluated various solutions. They agreed that the best solution would be to hire a General Manager, someone with good managerial skills and experience running a factory (the company did not have a General Manager at that time). Mr. S did this and the company's performance and profits improved significantly.

Eight years later Mr. S has developed health problems and recognizes that he needs to plan for when he will be unable to work. His two sons are both too young to run the business. Mr. S thought he might sell the company to an outside buyer, but over the years he has developed respect for and trust in the General Manager. Now Mr. S's plan is to set up a Trust through which the General Manager will run the company until he retires, at which point Mr. S's sons will be old enough to take control and can either decide to continue operating the company or sell it.

Mr. T, a serial entrepreneur, bought a company that was receiving more than 150 customer complaints each month. They were losing customers and morale at the company was terrible. Mr. T hired James C., a management consultant, to improve the company's operations.

James C. instituted an eight-step process that identified a host of issues and put in place a program to address these challenges. The primary tool was training the employees to provide exceptional customer service. Every employee attended a four-hour workshop to improve their skills in this area.

After three months the customer complaints had stopped completely. Customers were coming back and morale had turned around. Over the next three months the company continued to receive wonderful letters from the customers about the great customer service their employees were providing.

A mere two months later, because the company was now so successful, Mr. T was able to sell this company to a new owner and moved on to his next project.

The idea that your company may need to go through some changes or may need improvement in order to transition successfully may not be appealing to you. It suggests that what you have been doing as your company's owner is less than perfect. And no one likes to be criticized or made to feel that what they have done is less than perfect!

But another way to look at this issue is to think of it as a strategic question about the future of your company. As owner and CEO of your company you have the responsibility to think strategically about its long-term future. A key issue for you to think about strategically is the following:

How can my company thrive as a result of going through the transition to new ownership?

Some of the questions that can help you think about this issue:

- What changes do I need to make to my company, so it can run successfully without me?

- What special strengths does my company have?
- What weaknesses does my company have?
- What changes do I need to make to the company, so it will have value for and will be attractive to a new owner?
- What changes do I need to make to the company now, so it will bring me the future income I will need when it is under new ownership?

Because the ways in which you run your company may have become habitual, even automatic, it may be difficult for you to think about these issues or come up with innovative answers to these questions. Or even if you recognize that your company's operations could be improved or that its bottom line could be increased, you may not know where to begin to make these changes.

Effective CEOs not only think strategically about the future of their companies, they also recognize when they do not have the expertise to solve a particular problem, or when their viewpoint has become so narrow that it's difficult for them to think "outside the box." When that occurs, they need to call in competent outside support to help them expand their thinking and find successful new approaches.

Bringing in a Fresh Perspective

The challenge of improving your company so it can transition more successfully is an issue that will definitely benefit from a fresh perspective. A professional advisor who has experience in analyzing why companies are not living up to their full potential and expertise in helping them grow can provide the strategies your company needs now to increase its value in preparation for the Business Transition Process.

The case studies above describe some of the ways in which advisors with expertise in business improvement can help owners increase the value of their companies, preparing them for successful transitions.

Why Should You Improve the Value of Your Company as Part of the Business Transition Process?

Here are five reasons for improving your company's operations and increasing its bottom line as part of preparing it to transition successfully:

1. To appeal to the highest quality new owner, you want your company to be attractive and have value for this new owner.

2. The more value your company has, the more money you can get for it through the Business Transition Process.

3. Improving your company's operations now will increase its potential for continued success in the future (under your leadership, and under a new owner).

4. If you are counting on future payments from the company's future profits to support your future lifestyle, improving it now will help ensure that the company will continue successfully after you have left.

5. If the new owner lacks some skills or experience in running a company, you are providing them with a better foundation for success by improving the company before you transfer it to them.

For all these reasons, it will be to your benefit to improve your company's value and operations. Types of advisors who can help with this goal include Management Consultants, Business Improvement Specialists, Marketing and Sales Consultants, COOs-for-hire, and CFOs-for-hire.

CHAPTER 11

Your Collaborative "Dream Team": Working Together to Help You Achieve Your Goals

Twenty-five years ago Mr. U started a small retail appliance company that he grew to three locations in two states, with a wholesale unit, an active home contractor supply unit and annual revenues exceeding $1.3 million. He also owned the real estate where his businesses were located.

Prompted by the recent death of a family member, this very healthy middle-aged Baby Boomer owner resolved to get his financial affairs in order and began working with Stephen S., a personal financial planner, to create his future financial plans. Mr. U wanted to increase his retirement income, minimize taxes on his retirement portfolio withdrawals and leave a financial legacy for his adult children. He also wanted to retire from his company in 3 to 5 years.

Based on his lifestyle and future income needs, it became clear that Mr. U was in the financially enviable position of never needing to use all the money he had accumulated in his various investment and retirement accounts. But even though he was looking forward to retiring, he had not thought strategically about a succession plan.

Mr. U was assuming that a relative might take over the business, but he lacked a clear plan for transitioning to a new owner and he had not done a valuation of his business. Depending on the valuation, his lack of planning might potentially trigger a steep estate tax that could place his company at risk and put his heirs' financial legacy in jeopardy. With the encouragement of his financial planner, Mr. U began the next part of the planning process – to have a business valuation done for his company and develop a clear succession plan with his other family members.

Who should help you create and implement your Business Transition Strategic Plan?

Just as you need to create a detailed, comprehensive written Personal Transition Plan for your personal future in order to assure that you achieve it successfully, you also need a detailed, comprehensive written plan for your Business Transition Process.

A successful Business Transition Strategic Plan should cover a range of business, personal and financial issues. For example, it should include key issues such as:

- Your future personal financial needs.
- How much money do you need or want from your company by transferring it to new ownership (your Financial Transition Goal)?
- Other personal, financial and business goals that you want to achieve through the Business Transition Process.
- Is the current value of your company enough to meet your Financial Transition Goal?
- An evaluation of your company's readiness for transition, and a strategy for improving your company's readiness.
- How can you increase the value of your company so transferring it to new ownership will provide you with the money you want?
- Who would be the best new owner for your company?
- A strategy for transferring your company successfully to that new owner.
- A strategy for minimizing personal and business taxes incurred during the Business Transition Process.
- etc. etc. etc.

Someone has to gather and analyze all the relevant information to create your Business Transition Strategic Plan, then your plan needs to be implemented.

You, the owner, do not have the time or the many diverse types of expertise to create this comprehensive plan all by yourself – but you must be strategically involved with the creation of this plan because it is all about how to achieve your needs and goals.

You also do not have the time or the diverse types of expertise to implement the many different aspects of this plan all by yourself – but you must be strategically involved through the various steps of its implementation because this is all about you, your company and your future.

You rely on various types of professional advisors to help you run your business successfully. You also need to call on specific advisors to help you successfully create and implement your Business Transition Strategic Plan.

These advisors must work together as a team to help you create, assess, implement, reassess, refine and continue implementing your Business Transition Strategic Plan. They will be your Transition Advisory Team.

Your Transition Advisory Team: Advisors with Whom Owners Already Work

The professional advisors you already rely on, such as your personal financial planner or investment advisor, your CPA and your business attorney, will remain a key part of your transition advisory team.

But while these advisors are skilled at planning your personal finances and helping you run your business successfully, they may have little or no experience in helping owners plan for or implement the Business Transition Process. That's why your Transition Advisory Team also needs to include additional advisors, with the relevant skills and experience to help you create and implement your Business Transition Strategic Plan successfully.

You rely on various types of professional advisors to help you run your business successfully. You also need to call on specific advisors to help you successfully create and implement your Business Transition Strategic Plan. These advisors must work together as your Collaborative Transition Advisory Team.

Your Transition Advisory Team: Four Key Types of Transition Advisors

Figure 11-A graphically depicts the four key ways in which the members of your Transition Advisory Team can help you achieve a successful personal and business transition.

Figure 11-A

Four Key Ways Your Transition Advisors Can Help You Achieve a Successful Personal and Business Transition Process

Make it better

Make it happen

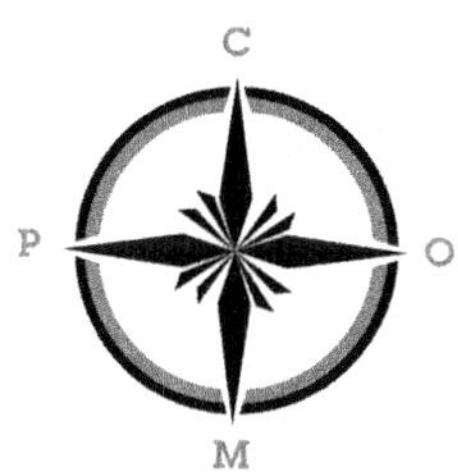

Make it matter

Make it last

<u>Make it matter</u>: An STPI-trained Transition Planning Consultant can help you reflect on what is truly important to you, so you can create meaningful personal and business transition goals that will guide your Business Transition Process and allow you to move on to a purposeful and satisfying new life. (See Chapter 12.)

<u>Make it better</u>: Many kinds of advisors can help you improve your business and make it more valuable to a new owner. Advisors who can help you achieve this outcome include:

- a Management Consultant
- a Sales or Marketing Consultant
- a Business Improvement Specialist

- a COO-for-hire
- a CFO-for-hire
- etc.

Make it happen: Professional advisors who can ensure that your company is transferred successfully to new ownership include:

- your CPA
- your Business Attorney
- an M&A Attorney
- an M&A Advisor
- an Investment Banker
- an ESOP Attorney
- etc.

Make it last: These advisors can ensure that the new wealth you get from transferring your company to new ownership will last as long as you need it:

- a Personal Financial Planner
- a Wealth Management or Investment Advisor
- an Estate Planning Attorney
- a 1031 Exchange Advisor
- a Business Insurance Advisor
- etc.

Note: A Business Insurance Advisor can assess insurance types and coverage for you and your company, update existing insurance policies and prepare a contingency plan, prepare for an owner's retirement or an owner's or partner's death, provide Key Person insurance and Buy-Sell insurance. They also offer life insurance policies that can provide immediately available funds so the company's operating expenses are covered until a Buy-Sell agreement is implemented.

Creating Your Collaborative "Dream Team" of Transition Advisors

Each of the advisors who works with you may be highly skilled and qualified in their own area of expertise. But you are not going to get the best results if you consult with each advisor separately. If they are working in isolation from each other (a "silo" approach), each advisor may have their own agenda or their own isolated knowledge base, and they may give you conflicting advice and information.

An owner who gets conflicting advice from isolated advisors can end up confused and discouraged, may make poor decisions or even choose to back out of the Business Transition Process. That's why you need to bring your advisors together so they can work as a collaborative team – and you need to designate someone to coordinate them.

An owner who gets conflicting advice from their advisors can end up confused and discouraged, may make poor decisions or may even choose to back out of the Business Transition Process. That's why, to assure that you get the best possible advice and support from your transition advisors, you need to bring them together so they can work as a collaborative team.

Your Dream Team of transition advisors needs someone to coordinate its various members, to make sure that each member is able to give the very best of their particular expertise and that all the members of your team are using their diverse skills to achieve the same goal – to help you accomplish your personal, business and financial transition goals.

Should you be your team's coordinator? The answer is "No." You already have plenty to do, keeping your business running day-to-day during the transition process, improving the business as needed, and making your personal preparations for leaving. You personally should not try to coordinate your transition advisory team in addition to everything else you are already doing.

That's why you need to designate a qualified individual who will officially coordinate the activities of the members of your Dream Team.

Choosing a Coordinator for Your Transition Advisory Team: A Lead Advisor

Your Dream Team needs a "point-person"/coordinator (sometimes referred to as a "quarterback") to coordinate the activities of your various transition advisors.

This coordinator is someone who will work closely with both you and the members of your transition advisory team to:

> Make sure that your transition goals are clear, and are clearly understood by the members of your Transition Advisory Team.
>
> Make sure that all your team members are using their skills and expertise to help you achieve your goals.
>
> Maintain regular communication among all the members of your Transition Advisory Team, so they can coordinate their diverse efforts and expertise to help you achieve your goals.

Maintain regular communication between you and your advisory team throughout the Business Transition Process, as your Business Transition Strategic Plan is being created and implemented.

Assure that you and the members of your Dream Team can respond effectively to new developments, and can work collaboratively to help you revise your plan if needed during the course of your Business Transition Process.

Owners usually choose this team coordinator through one of the following two methods:

1. Designate one of your advisors – someone you already know and trust, such as your CPA – to coordinate your Transition Advisory Team. This person becomes your "Lead Advisor."

2. Or engage a professional advisor who specializes in helping owners achieve a successful business transition, to coordinate your advisory team and overall Transition Process (see below).

You can choose one of your advisors – someone you already know and trust – as your "Lead Advisor." This Lead Advisor will coordinate the other members of your Transition Advisory Team as they participate in helping you create and implement your Business Transition Strategic Plan.

If you decide to choose one of your current advisors to act as your Lead Advisor and coordinate your Transition Advisory Team, this individual should be an advisor who is:

- Skilled at working with and coordinating the input of other people.
- Knowledgeable about the overall Business Transition Process.

- Committed to making sure that all members of your Dream Team are using their skills and expertise to help you achieve your personal, business and financial goals.

Your Lead Advisor should convene regular meetings for you and your Dream Team. During these meetings each advisor reports on what they have done since the previous meeting to further your transition goals, raises questions they may have, and you and the other advisors can offer information or suggestions to help move the process along.

Regular meetings for you and your Transition Advisory Team provide the opportunity for reporting on the implementation of your Business Transition Strategic Plan, assessing, refining and changing it as needed, then continuing with its improved implementation.

Choosing a Professional Coordinator for Your Transition Advisory Team: A Chief Transition Officer

Your other option is to hire a professional advisor who specializes in helping owners achieve their business transitions.

This professional advisor will analyze your company and situation, create a comprehensive, detailed Business Transition Strategic Plan for you and your company, then will oversee the implementation of this plan by working with you during the Business Transition Process and coordinating the activities of your Transition Advisory Team members.

Professionals who specialize in helping business owners achieve their business transitions have a variety of professional titles. For example, they may call themselves an:

- Exit planner
- Business transition specialist

- Management consultant

We at STPI refer to a professional advisor who creates your business transition plan and oversees its implementation as your "Chief Transition Officer" or "CTrO."

You can think of a professional advisor who creates your transition plan and oversees its implementation as your "Chief Transition Officer" or "CTrO." Your CTrO might be a qualified individual professional, or even a small group of professional advisors who work together as a team to perform the function of a CTrO.

Your CTrO might be a qualified individual professional, or even a small group of professional advisors who work together as a team to perform the function of a CTrO.

Here is an example of a small team of professionals who work together to carry out the functions of a Chief Transition Officer. This team first works with an owner to analyze and create a transition plan that meets the owner's personal, business and financial needs, then they coordinate the company's employees and the owner's other advisors to implement this plan.

> "MW Consultants" is a three-person firm that helps owners plan and implement their personal and business transition process. The three partners – a wealth engineer, an executive leadership advisor/team-building strategist, and a business improvement specialist – work together as a team to design transition plans for the owners and the companies, facilitate the plans' implementation and coordinate the activities of various advisors so they are working together to help owners achieve their transition goals.

> The MW team begins by identifying all the professional advisors the owner is currently working with and reaches out to each advisor to affirm the importance of collaboration for the owner's best interests. After performing a detailed assessment which evaluates both the company's Business Readiness and the owner's Emotional and Personal Financial Readiness for transition, the MW team develops a transition plan for the owner and the company.
>
> As needed, the MW team brings in additional specialists, such as experts in marketing, sales, a business attorney or other business professionals to improve the company's readiness, and accountants, insurance specialists, financial planners or other professionals to help with the owner's personal financial readiness.
>
> Although various professional advisors may need to work individually with the owner throughout the transition process, MW partners act as the overall facilitators of the transition process, to ensure that all these advisors are working in a coordinated manner within the framework of the transition plan.

And here's an example of how this team worked with two owners to help them transition successfully:

> Mr. and Mrs. V had run their company for 25 years. They were burned out and stressed. As a result, they wanted to be out of

the business in the next 3 to 5 years, but didn't know how. They were heavily involved in running the company, their employees were not communicating with each other, they were uncertain that all their efforts would result in them being able to sell the business, and their financial future was filled with doubt. They were referred to "MW Consultants," a firm that specializes in helping owners achieve successful personal and business transitions.

The MW team created a coherent transition plan to maximize business value, extricate the owners from the rigors of running the business day to day, and help achieve the longer term goal of transitioning both the owners and the company. MW then facilitated the plan's implementation. They worked with the owners to improve the company's internal operations; coordinated outsourced marketing and sales efforts into alignment; gave the company's management team new direction, responsibility and accountability, which allowed Mr. and Mrs. V to decrease their personal involvement in the business; and the company's bottom line began to increase. In parallel, MW worked with current and new personal financial advisors to create a plan for Mr. and Mrs. V that improved their personal finances independent from the sale of the company; and facilitated their various advisors in working together toward the coordinated goal of helping Mr. and Mrs. V leave successfully.

As Mr. and Mrs. V moved through the process, they began to see new possibilities for their future. They began to view each other as a couple again, rather than merely business partners. Within a year of working with MW Consultants, the company has achieved tremendous revenue increases and Mr. and Mrs. V have a renewed financial foundation and plan that greatly enhances the chances of selling their company if they want to, but also gives them other transition options to choose from, according to their own liking and timeframe.

How Transactional Advisors and Transition Planning Consultants Work Together

Many transactional (business and financial) advisors are now recognizing that they need to collaborate with transition advisors who will help the owner become mentally and emotionally ready to engage in transition planning and implementation.

Here are three ways through which this can be done.

1. A transactional advisor who recognizes that an owner who approaches them is not really emotionally ready to plan and implement their business transition may refer that owner to an STPI-trained Transition Planning Consultant, who will help the owner clarify their goals and become mentally and emotionally ready to think seriously about moving on.

2. A transactional advisor (or a firm of transactional advisors) may have a collaborative relationship with a Transition Planning Consultant, whom they call upon when needed to work with an owner who is not emotionally ready for the Business Transition Process.

3. A firm that provides some aspect of transition planning or implementation, such as a personal financial planning firm or a business intermediary, may have one of their staff members trained by STPI as a Transition Planning Consultant, so they can help owners who are not emotionally ready for the transition process become mentally and emotionally prepared to let go of their company and move on to their new future.

Here is a case study about how a firm of transactional advisors collaborated with a Transition Planning Consultant to help owners transition successfully.

For 32 years Mr. and Mrs. W built their company, which sold and installed industrial air-quality systems, and the business was now bringing in $5 million in annual sales revenue. Their son, who also worked in the company, was extremely successful at bringing in new business and felt ready to take over ownership, but his parents were not ready to think about leaving.

Mr. and Mrs. W had several serious concerns about their future. They worried that if they passed ownership to their son, their retirement would be financially dependent on his future success in running the company. They also had absolutely no idea what they would do with their lives once they stopped working.

Their CPA, who was aware of their dilemma, recommended they consult with "A.L. Wealth Management Associates," who could help them design the internal transfer to their son, plan their finances so they could retire successfully, and also help them design a new life for themselves. Mr. and Mrs. W agreed to work with the A.L. team.

A.L. Associates had a collaborative relationship with an STPI-trained Transition Planning Consultant. They referred Mr. and Mrs. W to the TPC, who helped them deal with their anxieties and fears about leaving, then worked with them to help them think about what was important to them and what they wanted to do in the next stage of their lives. With the TPC's assistance, Mr. and Mrs. W created a plan for future activities they wanted to do together as well as things they wanted to do independent of each other.

Now that they had an exciting strategic plan for their future, Mr. and Mrs. W felt motivated to leave their company. They met with members of the A.L team, who used this future lifestyle plan to design the best investment vehicles for achieving their personal and financial objectives.

During their work with the TPC, the couple had also explored various options for new ownership and decided that the best strategy was to transition the company to their son. Their CPA then prepared a business plan, created cash flow projections and did a preliminary estimate of the value of their company. It was determined that they should hire a management consultant to help them improve the operation of the business so they could leave with the greatest amount of money when they moved on.

> After all their goals had been articulated, financial needs identified and a financial plan created, an attorney working with the CPA and the A.L. team prepared an estate plan consistent with Mr. and Mrs. W's transition plan. This collaborative model – which allowed these owners to deal with both the Head and Heart issues of the Transition Process – resulted in a successful business succession.

For more about how STPI-trained Transition Planning Consultants help owners become mentally and emotionally ready for the transition process and help them plan and implement a fulfilling new life, see Chapter 12.

Finding the Transition Advisors for Your Dream Team

One way to find transition advisors who can help you design and implement your Business Transition Strategic Plan is by asking your friends and colleagues for recommendations.

Because STPI's mission is to help owners transition successfully, our website, www.successfultransitionplanning.com also includes an interactive community of the many different types of professional advisors who can help you with creating and implementing every aspect of your personal and business transition plans. (See "Advisory Network" on STPI's website.)

The professional advisors listed on STPI's website are not only skilled in their distinct areas of expertise; they also have experience with the transition planning and implementation process.

STPI's website is designed so you can learn about any of these advisors with no obligation on your part. After reading profiles of advisors on

STPI's website, you can then go search their LinkedIn and Facebook profiles, their blogs, articles, newsletters, videos, and more. You may also visit the advisors' own websites to learn more about them.

When you have decided on advisors who interest you, you should then meet with them in person to learn more about what they have to offer and decide if they are right for you.

STPI will continue to add advisors to this community.

CHAPTER 12

Finding Your New Owner: A Head and Heart Approach

Harry Y. grew his Connecticut-based photocopy equipment company until it was serving numerous customers throughout southern New England. Several years ago a big national chain entered the region and began squeezing Harry out. They undercut his prices, took away his customers, then offered to buy his company. Although Harry had no intention of retiring, he knew he could not compete with the chain, and since their buy-out offer was very generous he sold them his company. Now what?

For several months Harry hung around the house aimlessly. Suddenly he decided what to do with his unexpected wealth. He announced to his wife Linda that they were going to move to Las Vegas because he loved "the buzz" of that glamorous city. Linda did not want to leave her friends and family, but after months of constant pressure from Harry she finally agreed.

In Las Vegas, Harry spent his days hanging around the clubs, while Linda tried to live a normal life. After a year of this, Linda announced that she had only made two friends, both of whom had moved away. She was fed up and was going to get a divorce and move back to her family in Connecticut. Harry was distraught. He didn't want to lose Linda, but he had no idea how to change his lifestyle. The two of them moved back to Connecticut, where Harry continued his aimless life.

Meanwhile, some of Harry's friends were doing Personal Transition Planning with an STPI-trained consultant. Knowing that Harry needed help, they urged him to work with this Transition Planning Consultant to design a new life for himself. In desperation, Harry agreed.

Working with the TPC and STPI's materials, Harry began to design a comprehensive and meaningful plan for his future, which also included Linda's needs and preferences. During the course of the program Harry mentioned that he loved pretzels and had always wanted to have an outdoor pretzel cart. This became an important part of his new plan.

Harry is now having a ball selling pretzels to tourists on the New England seacoast. A few months ago the TPC visited Harry

> at his pretzel cart. Harry threw his arms around the TPC and told him, "In two months you helped me straighten out what it took me two years to screw up."

Many people have asked me how STPI came into being and how I created its unique Integrative Transition Planning approach that helps an owner work with both the Head and Heart issues of transition planning. Here's my story.

Back in 1980 I founded Designer Orthopedics, a cost-containment company that sold high-quality surgical instruments and orthopedic devices to the medical and healthcare industries. Within a few years I had built DO into a multi-million dollar business supplying hospitals all across the U.S.

Although I enjoyed the status and material success that DO brought, I wanted to do more with my life. I wanted to find a way to transform organizations, to help the people who lead and work in them achieve lives that would be both more successful and more meaningful and empowered.

Since DO's headquarters was in Boston, it was easy for me to cross the river into Cambridge a few hours each week to study at the Harvard Divinity School. I spent two years as the "Div School's" first "Special Student," which meant I was there not to become a theologian or clergyperson, but to deepen and expand my understanding of philosophical and spiritual issues. My special area of study was Comparative Religions; my goal was to integrate the latest Western scientific research in physics and cosmology – research into the nature of the universe – with Eastern spiritual philosophies. I also wanted to understand why "positive thinking" – a foundation of business success –

does not always work, and I wanted to find a more effective approach for achieving personal and business success.

My studies at Harvard, along with additional research I continued afterwards on my own, led me to develop an innovative process for integrating Head and Heart issues to achieve personal and business success – an approach that I call "the Balanced Paradigm." (For more about the Balanced Paradigm, see Jack Beauregard, *The Power of Balance: Seven Principles for Transforming Mind, Spirit, and Self*, Innervision Press, 2001.)

I then started a new company, Innervisions Associates, which for over 20 years has developed and presented transformative training programs to leaders and their organizations in business, healthcare and education. Our programs, based on the Balanced Paradigm, have helped hundreds of leaders learn how to expand their thinking for both increased personal empowerment and organizational success.

In the mid-1990s Innervisions Associates began to work with firms going through the Mergers-and-Acquisitions process, to help them integrate their divergent corporate cultures. To my great surprise, I saw over and over again that after having sold their companies to other firms, these former owners were completely unprepared to leave their ownership roles and move on to a new life. Most of these owners who had just sold their firms had put no thought into what they would do with their lives after they were no longer owners, and they were now facing empty, depressing futures.

From my many years creating transformative Innervisions programs and applying the Balanced Paradigm to help business leaders integrate Head and Heart issues for increased personal and business success, I was able to understand that these owners I was now meeting were completely emotionally unprepared to think about leaving. And I realized that this pattern was common to many business owners, who did not want to think about or plan for a new future in which they would no longer be running their companies.

I also realized that with a growing wave of Baby Boomers approaching retirement age, there would soon be hundreds of thousands of Baby Boomer business owners who should be thinking about moving on with their lives, but who would need help doing this. Here was an extraordinary opportunity for sharing the uniquely transformative Head and Heart methods I had developed with a broad new audience of Baby Boomer business owners, to help them transition successfully out of their companies and into personally fulfilling and meaningful new futures.

I began working one-on-one with business owners and senior executives who were facing future personal and business transitions. One of the most important principles I learned through this work was that in order for an owner to feel emotionally comfortable and be able to think clearly about leaving their current position, they <u>first</u> had to create an exciting, comprehensive and detailed picture of <u>the new life</u> they wanted to move into – and they had to develop a concrete implementation plan for how they would move into that new life. Only then would they be emotionally comfortable with the idea of moving on.

After several years of working one-on-one with business owners and other high-powered businesspeople going through transitions, I had created a new system of programs that could guide a businessperson facing transition through the entire mental/emotional readiness and personal planning process. I then realized that because there are now so many Baby Boomers who could benefit from this new service, I could also train other professional advisors to present the programs I had created.

I founded STPI – the Successful Transition Planning Institute – to educate Baby Boomer business owners and other high-powered businesspeople about this new approach to transition planning. And I created a new career opportunity – the "Transition Planning Consultant" – for professional advisors who my colleagues and I at STPI now train to use STPI's unique Integrative Transition Planning programs and methods with Baby Boomer businesspeople preparing for transitions.

Transition Planning Consultants and STPI's Integrative Transition Planning Programs

STPI-trained Transition Planning Consultants use STPI's Integrative Head and Heart methods and materials with owners to help them become mentally and emotionally ready to do transition planning and help them think through and design their personal, business and financial goals.

A Transition Planning Consultant (TPC) is a professional advisor who works with high-powered business owners, and who wants to include this dynamic new skill set among the services they offer. For example, a TPC might also be a Personal Financial Planner, an Executive Coach, a Management Consultant or other highly skilled professional advisor who now wants to help owners work with the Head and Heart issues of the Transition Process.

My colleagues and I at STPI have turned our unique Integrative Transition Planning approach into three programs – THINK, LIVE and DECIDE – that a TPC uses to work one-on-one with an owner. Our methodology allows the owner to take a businesslike approach to thinking strategically about not only business and financial issues, but also about their personal life and emotions related to the Transition Process.

A Transition Planning Consultant using STPI's programs with an owner uses a methodical, step-by-step approach based on the experiences and familiar thinking styles of business owners to help them feel comfortable thinking strategically about both the Head and Heart issues involved in the Transition Process. In addition to using facts, logic and sound business principles, this approach allows the owner to bring key aspects of their personal life into the process and helps them feel comfortable while becoming aware of and thinking strategically about their own emotions in relation to the prospect of transitioning out of their company and into a new future.

In Program 1-THINK, which is conducted in four weekly 90-minute sessions, the TPC helps the owner become personally and emotionally prepared for the Transition Process. The TPC helps the owner become aware of and learn how to transform emotional issues such as fear of an unknown future, self-identification with their role as owner, and feelings of loss about moving on – any or all of which may be preventing the owner from thinking clearly and creatively about new possibilities for their future. The owner also begins to think about creating their personal and financial transition goals.

In Program 2-LIVE, the TPC helps the owner design a completely personalized comprehensive plan for the new life they can't wait to live, along with a detailed implementation plan for each of their new life goals. The TPC also helps the owner become aware of their unique decision-making style, so they can use the unique strengths of that style to successfully create and implement their transition plans. The LIVE program is conducted in eight weekly 90-minute sessions and results in the owner's unique "Strategic Plan for Living an Exciting and Purposeful New Life." The LIVE program can be taken by an owner who is still considering whether or not they should leave their company and needs a plan for their new life before they are ready to think seriously and strategically about their business transition. Or (as in the case of Harry Y. above) the LIVE program can also be taken by an owner who has already left their company, but now needs a plan for a fulfilling and meaningful new life.

In Program 3-DECIDE, the TPC helps the owner analyze their options for new ownership and decide on the best new owner for their company. They also guide the owner in thinking about the personal, financial and business outcomes they want from the Business Transition Process; the various steps needed to implement these goals; and emotional issues which might develop during the Business Transition Process and how the owner can be prepared to deal with them. The DECIDE program also helps the owner plan for how they can assemble and work effectively with a Collaborative Team of Transition Advisors and how to choose the team's coordinator.

Taking Time Out to Focus on Yourself

STPI's Integrative Transition Planning system is powerful, practical and effective. It provides the owner with essential information about the business and financial issues involved in creating a successful Transition Process, and at the same time helps the owner reflect on how their personal dreams and emotions can shape a meaningful Transition Process and a fulfilling new life.

Through many years working with business owners going through various types of personal and business transitions, I discovered that something many owners deeply crave is simply the opportunity to talk about their life and the challenges they are facing with someone who understands and can listen non-judgmentally. Owners are not looking for therapy. What they want is to be able to share their stories with a qualified advisor who understands the business world, understands the unique issues faced by a business owner, and who is willing to take the time to listen caringly and appreciatively.

After reading this book, you may now want to work one-on-one with an STPI-certified Transition Planning Consultant. In fact, this may be the only opportunity you will have to simply sit back and reflect on your life and talk about what is truly meaningful to you – the only time in your life that you will be totally focused on who you are and what you want to do with your future. And by working with an STPI-trained Transition Planning Consultant, you will be talking about these deep issues with another intelligent businessperson, who will both listen to you caringly and non-judgmentally and will show you how to use your thoughts, feelings, dreams and values to create a successful Transition Plan and a meaningful new future for your life.

Many owners deeply crave the opportunity to simply talk about their life and the challenges they are facing with someone who understands and can listen non-judgmentally. STPI's Integrative Transition Planning programs and the Transition Planning Consultants trained by STPI can provide you with this opportunity.

(If you are interested in getting in touch with a professional who has been trained in STPI's methods, go to our website: www.successfultransitionplanning.com, and click on transition community.)

Finding Your New Owner – for Your Business, for Your Life

Many owners feel that they don't have time to think about the future. But one of the most important gifts you can give yourself is to take the time, now, to reflect more deeply on what is truly meaningful to you and explore the new possibilities about who you can be and what you can do in the next stage of your life.

As a Baby Boomer business owner, you are now facing the challenge of having to think about transitioning your business and moving on with your life. There is no better time than now to step back and look at your past accomplishments, then expand your thinking so you can create a new future for your company and a meaningful and exciting new life for yourself.

I hope that as a result of reading this book, you are now feeling excited and hopeful about the prospect of transferring your company to new ownership and moving on to a dynamic new future filled with new meaning and purpose.

The end of this book is <u>your</u> New Beginning. Get started!

Additional Resources

Are you a business owner? Here's how STPI will help you:

STPI's Three Stage Transition Planning System:

1. Thinking About Your Future
2. Planning Your Personal Financial Future
3. Planning Your Business Future

Successful Transition Planning Principles:

1. You must be mentally and emotionally ready to think about planning
2. You need to create two distinct plans: Personal and Business
3. You need to develop a clear vision of your new life first

STPI's Modular Programs

A methodical, businesslike, step-by-step approach that utilizes owners' thinking styles and experiences:

1. Strategic Thinking for Your Personal and Business Future
2. Living an Exciting New Life: Seven Strategic Steps for Creating Your Successful Personal Transition Plan
3. Deciding What to Do with Your Business and Creating a Successful Business Transition Strategy

To learn more about creating your new future contact STPI in Cambridge MA:

1.800.677.6715 | info@thenextransition.com

www.successfultransitonplanning.com

Facebook.com: nexttransition | Twitter.com: @nexttransition

Testimonials from clients who have taken STPI's Transition Programs:

"I worked with STPI to create a game plan for myself especially pertinent to my sixth decade. Using STPI's planning process, I worked through a number of issues including where I want to live, how I want work and career to factor into my future, and hobbies and volunteer activities I want to experience and peruse…the written plan provides peace of mind and a touchstone to ensure I am using my time and energy to fulfill my vision and live by my values."

Joni Youngwirth – Managing Principal of a financial broker-dealer company

"STPI helped me build a bridge from my former role as a business owner, to my transitional role as a member of the management team of the acquiring business, to my future goal—a productive and successful balance between work I enjoy and a satisfying personal life. I can recommend STPI without reservation if you are facing challenges and change."

S. Z. Harris – Founder & Former Owner of a medical reimbursement software company

"I enjoyed the time [working with STPI]. Got my mind and thinking focused. The sessions got me unstuck. It has been 5 months since I went part time and as of Friday I am done with [my former company... I seem to be busier than ever. I can't seem to do all that I want to…I have been following the plan STPI and I outlined and could not be happier."

Larry Shwartz – Former Co-owner of a large food distribution company

"The Personal Transition Planning experience was not only positive, it was also provocative since it made me think. Conversations in the sessions allowed me to get a clear vision of myself, understand what I wanted to do and be able to forge a clear path for my life."

Sam Palestine – Former Co-Owner of an office supply company

More Transition Planning Resources

John M. Leonetti, *Exiting Your Business, Protecting Your Wealth: A Strategic Guide for Owners and Their Advisors*, John Wiley & Sons, Inc., 2008.

A comprehensive discussion that covers both transactional and emotional issues involved in transition planning. Especially good explanations of the various options for new ownership (internal succession, ESOPs, selling to an outside buyer, private equity recap, etc.) why to choose which option, and how to work with a collaborative advisory team.

John H. Brown, *How To Run Your Business So You Can Leave It In Style*, Business Enterprise Press/Business Enterprise Institute Inc., (revised 4th edition) 2009.

A clear, comprehensive explanation of the major options for new ownership, advantages and disadvantages of each option and the transactional issues involved in exit planning. Provides detailed information about legal, tax and other key technical and financial issues. An entire chapter discusses programs for keeping employees motivated during the transition process.

Wayne Vanwyck, *The Business Transition Crisis: Plan Your Succession Now and Beat the Biggest Business Selloff in History*, BPS Books/Bastian Publishing Services Ltd., 2010.

This book will help prepare you for transitioning your company by showing you how to explore new possibilities for your personal future; prepare yourself, your employees and your company for transition; and create and implement a business transition plan that will increase your company's valuation when you are ready to leave.

Thomas William Deans, Ph.D., *Every Family's Business: 12 Common Sense Questions to Protect Your Wealth*, Détente Financial Press, 2008.

Whether or not your family members are directly involved with your company, every privately-held business is a family business. This book shows business owners how to open up family communication on what to do with their business, discusses strategies for preserving your family's wealth by keeping the company, by selling it, why not to pass your company on to your children, and how to transfer it within the family successfully,

John Warrillow, *Built To Sell: Creating a Business That Can Thrive Without You*, Portfolio/Penguin, 2011.

Most owners find it difficult to step out of the picture because they've built a business that relies too heavily on their personal involvement. This comprehensive yet entertaining book explains how you can create a company that will thrive even when you are no longer involved in it.

John H. Brown with Kevin M. Short, *Cash Out, Move On: Get Top Dollar and More Selling Your Business*, Business Enterprise Press/ Business Enterprise Institute, 2008.

This book focuses on why and how to sell your company in order to get the most money and be able to move most quickly into your new life. A clear, comprehensive explanation of both the strategic and transactional issues involved in selling your company successfully, and thorough descriptions of the various advisors who can help you prepare for and implement the sale.

Patricia M. Annino, *Women and Money: A Practical Guide to Estate Planning.* (Available from amazon.com)

How Baby Boomers Are Redefining Their Futures

J. Walker Smith and Ann Clurman, *Generation Ageless: How Baby Boomers are changing the way we live – and they're just getting started*, Collins, 2007.

John Charles Goldsmith, *The Long Baby Boom: An Optimistic Vision for a Graying Generation*, Johns Hopkins University Press, 2008.

Marjorie Zoet Bankson, *Creative Aging: Rethinking Retirement and Non-retirement in a Changing World*, Sky Light Paths, 2010.

Donald R. Haas, *How to Plan for Baby Boomers: Advisor's Guide to the New Retirement Model*, National Underwriter Co., 2007.

The New Paradigm in Health

Allen Luks with Peggy Payne, *The Healing Power of Doing Good*, iUniverse.com, 1991.

Alice D. Domar, Ph.D, and Henry Dreher, *Healing Mind, Healthy Woman: Using the Mind-Body Connection to Manage Stress and Take Control of Your Life*, Delta Trade Paperbacks, 1996.

Robert M. Sapolsky, *Why Zebras don't get Ulcers*, Holt Paperbacks, 2004.

Stephen Post, Ph.D. and Jill Neimark, *Why Good Things Happen to Good People: How to Live a Longer, Healthier, Happier Life by the Simple Act of Giving*, Broadway Books, 2007.

John T. Cacioppo and William Patrick, *Loneliness: Human Nature and the Need for Social Connections*, W.W. Norton & Company, 2008.

John Kabat-Zinn, Ph.D., *Full Catastrophe Living: Using the Wisdom of your Body and Mind to Face Stress, Pain, and Illness*, Delta Trade Paperbacks, 2009.

"The reason loneliness may be bad for your health," *The Economist*, February 26, 2011, p. 87.

"Warding off dementia," (article about how engaging in social activities can reduce the risk of developing Alzheimer's), *The Week*, May 13, 2011, p. 21.

The New Paradigm of Healthy Aging

Linda L. Beeson and Mary Jane Dugan, *The Body-Mind-Spirit Links to Healthy Aging*, Edwin Mellen Press, 2002.

Andrew Weil, M.D., *Healthy Aging: A Lifelong Guide to your Physical and Spiritual Well-Being*, Alfred A. Knopf, 2005.

Linda J. Altoonian, *Living Agelessly: Answers to your most common questions about aging gracefully*, Diamedica, 2009.

Brent Agin, *Healthy Aging for Dummies*, Thorndike Press, 2009.

Robert N. Butler, M.D., *The Longevity Prescription: The 8 Proven Keys to a Long, Healthy Life*, Avery, 2010.

Gene Cohen, M.D., Ph.D., *The Mature Mind: The Positive Power of the Aging Brain*, Perseus Book Group, 2005.

Alvaro Fernandez and Dr. Elkhonon Goldberg, *The Sharpbrains Guide to Brain Fitness*, Sharpbrains, Inc., 2009.

Richard M. Restak, *Think Smart: A Neuroscientist's Prescription for Improving Your Brain's Performance*, Riverhead Books, 2009.

National Institute on Aging, *Fitness over Fifty: An Exercise Guide from the National Institute on Aging*, Healthy Living Books, 2006.

Walter H. Ettinger, M.D., Brenda S. Wright, Ph.D. and Steven N. Blair Ph.D., *Fitness After 50: Add years to your life and life to your years*, Human Kinetics, 2006.

Michael Fekete, *Strength Training for Seniors: How to Rewind your Biological Clock*, Hunter House, 2006.

Vonda Wright, M.D., *Fitness after 40: How to Stay Strong at any Age*, AMACOM, 2009.

Michael Gloth, *Fit at Fifty and Beyond: A Balanced Exercise and Nutrition Program*, Diamedica, 2009.

Ordering Information

Finding Your New Owner can be purchased at any on-line book retailer and may be ordered at almost any bookstore in the US. It may also be available in the UK and Australia – check your favorite on-line retailer there.

Bulk Purchase Options

A paperback version is available for bulk purchase by advisors:

- Use as gifts to your clients
- Promotional gift to attract prospects
- Minimum order is only ten copies

Please visit our website to learn more:

www.successfultransitionplanning.com
Click on "Learning Center"

You may also contact us at:

Successful Transition Planning Institute
One Mifflin Place, Harvard Square
Cambridge, MA 02138
Phone: 1.800.677.6715
info@successfultransitionplanning.com

Facebook "Like" us and comment – enter "Finding Your New Owner" in top Search box on www.facebook.com

Twitter @nexttransition

LinkedIn If you are an experienced advisor to business owners, executives and professionals, you may wish to join our LinkedIn Group: Successful Transition Planning Institute

CPSIA information can be obtained at www.ICGtesting.com
Printed in the USA
BVOW11s1913030316

438992BV00001B/4/P

9 780983 631101